EVERY
DAY I READ

From the internationally bestselling author of *Welcome to the Hyunam-dong Bookshop* comes a warm and reflective collection of essays about reading, language and life.

Why do we read? What is it that we hope to take away from the intimate, personal experience of reading for pleasure?

Rarely do we ask these profound, expansive questions of ourselves and of our relationship to the joy of reading. But in this gentle, philosophical collection celebrating books, reading and language, Hwang Bo-reum doesn't just tell us; she shows us what living a life immersed in reading means.

Every Day I Read provides many quiet moments for introspection and reflection and encourages book-lovers to explore what reading means to each of us. While this is a book about books, at its heart it is an attitude to life. Readers and non-readers alike will take something away from it, including a treasure trove of book recommendations blended seamlessly within.

EVERY DAY I READ

HWANG BO-REUM

Translated by Shanna Tan

BLOOMSBURY PUBLISHING
LONDON · OXFORD · NEW YORK · NEW DELHI · SYDNEY

BLOOMSBURY PUBLISHING
Bloomsbury Publishing Plc
50 Bedford Square, London, WC1B 3DP, UK
Bloomsbury Publishing Ireland Limited
29 Earlsfort Terrace, Dublin 2, D02 AY28, Ireland

BLOOMSBURY, BLOOMSBURY PUBLISHING and the Diana logo
are trademarks of Bloomsbury Publishing Plc

First published in 2021 in South Korea by A Certain Book
매일 읽겠습니다 © Hwang Bo-reum 2021, 2025
English Translation © Shanna Tan 2025

English translation rights arranged with Bloomsbury Publishing Plc through BC
Agency, Seoul and Rogers, Coleridge & White Ltd, London

Hwang Bo-reum is identified as the author of this work in accordance
with the Copyright, Designs and Patents Act 1988

A catalogue record for this book is available from the British Library

ISBN: HB: 978-1-5266-9280-1; TPB: 978-1-0372-0092-2;
EBOOK: 978-1-5266-9338-9; EPDF: 978-1-5266-9341-9

4 6 8 10 9 7 5 3

Typeset by Six Red Marbles India
Printed and bound in India by Thomson Press India Ltd

To find out more about our authors and books visit www.bloomsbury.com
and sign up for our newsletters
For product-safety-related questions contact productsafety@bloomsbury.com

For sale in the Indian subcontinent only

Excerpt(s) from LETTERS TO FRIENDS, FAMILY, AND EDITORS by Franz Kafka,
translated by Richard and Clara Winston, translation copyright © 1977 by Penguin
Random House LLC. Used by permission of Schocken Books, an imprint of the
Knopf Doubleday Publishing Group, a division of Penguin Random House LLC.
All rights reserved

(c) Ivan Illich 1978
Reprinted by permission of Equinox Publishing Ltd

Quotation from *Selfish Gene* by Richard Dawkins on p. 154 reproduced
with permission of the Licensor through PLSclear

Grateful acknowledgement to the publishers of works by Geum Jung-yeon,
Mizumaru Anzai, and Jeong In-seong for their gratis permission to print
material in English translation for the first time

CONTENTS

CONTENTS

AUTHOR'S NOTE
Updated Edition

A little more courage,
a little less doubt

Back in 2017, when I was writing this book, I had a Post-it note stuck to my monitor:

How to Get Closer to Books

That'd been the working title of the book, and something that I've been thinking about – how do I deepen my relationship with reading? The thought set off a firework of questions in my mind: *If someone hasn't been reading for a while, should they start with a bestseller? Is it OK to put down a book midway if I'm struggling? Does reading give me answers to my worries or a boost of motivation on bad days? If I'm too busy to read, will setting a timer help me focus?*

I jotted them down one by one, soaking in the quiet joy of taking the first steps towards writing my first book – on my favourite topic, no less! Eventually, my publisher and I went with the title *Every Day I Read: 53 Ways to Get Closer to Books*, and we bundled a free weekly planner with every purchase.

Life didn't take a dramatic turn just because I became a published author. I still spend the bulk of my time reading and writing in the comfort of my room. But two things changed: first was my newfound identity as an author (albeit an unknown one), and second, the new experiences I gained as a result.

I was thrilled to receive emails and handwritten letters from readers. Reading their reviews filled me with gratitude. Book clubs were discussing my work, and I was torn between excitement and anxiety when invited to give talks. And for the first time, people addressed me as *jakka-nim* – an author. All of which I'd never have experienced had I not written a book.

But the realisation that I'm now a published author only truly hit home in an unexpected moment. One day I was writing at my desk when I happened to turn around and look at the hundreds of books on my shelves. There were life-changing books that shaped me into the person I am, books that I'd annotated in detail. I might not quite remember what some of them were about, but I'm sure somewhere, at some point, they had and will continue to exert a quiet influence on my life. Suddenly, a tingle spread in my chest.

Someone might also be reaching for my book at this very moment.

Three years have passed since this collection of essays was first published, and in between, I've put out two more books. But some things haven't changed. I'm still an unknown author and still reading, of course. I can't imagine otherwise. When I'm feeling a little down, or when I'm trying to understand something, whether it's about the bigger world out there, everyday life, about myself, or you, I turn to my shelves.

Books may not give me answers, but they nudge me towards the right direction. I keep their words close to my heart. Knowing that I'm not navigating life alone makes me feel a little more courageous, a little less unsure.

In preparation for this new edition, I revisited the essays for the first time in a while. Three years isn't a long time, but I found myself marvelling at how much I'd read 'back then'. Leafing through the pages transported me back to the days when I was fresh out of school, navigating the stress of my first job, the depression that followed, and the anxiety of chasing after my dreams. Amidst it all, books were steadfast companions, supporting me through all the highs and lows in life.

I still can't believe I wrote and published an essay collection spurred solely by my love for reading. I look up and cast a sweeping gaze at the library in my room.

What should I read today? Should I continue from where I've left a pencil slotted between the pages? Or the paperback that has just arrived in the post, or the book club picks on my TBR (to-be-read) stack?

I read every day. Because I'm bored, because I crave a story, because I feel a little empty. I read to understand what my friends are going through, to breathe some hope into life. But most importantly, I read because I love it. Every day I read, and I'll keep reading.

Hwang Bo-reum

INTRODUCTION

Take a break,
the world of books is waiting

Back in middle school, I used to walk to school with my friends. We were a bunch of noisy teenage girls, chatting away non-stop. Sometimes I'd tell them about a book I had read the night before, and on those days, the walk to school felt even shorter than usual. As I changed into my indoor slippers, I was already counting down to the last bell so that I could go home and pick up where I'd left off.

I loved thinking about books. I'd rest my chin on the table and let my thoughts drift to a different world. Those were my favourite moments of the day. I couldn't help it. The world of books was far more interesting than being glued to a hard plastic chair all day long.

I've always found it hard to conform to the so-called standards. Each time a teacher or an adult told me I shouldn't do this or that, I'd nod but let their words breeze past me. I refused to believe there was only one path in life. But contemplating the future was scary, and when my thoughts threatened to overwhelm me, I'd seek refuge for a couple of hours in the sanctuary of books.

When I think about books, I think about the cylindrical water cask in Edgar Allan Poe's short story 'A Descent into the Maelström'. In the story, a seaman recounts his experience of being caught in the treacherous whirlpool in the seas off Lofoten, Norway. With a diameter of more than two kilometres, the whirlpool swallowed everything in its vicinity and as the seaman was falling into the abyss, he recalled how he had seen at the shore objects that the whirlpool had sucked in and spat out. Everything was broken and splintered, save for the bobbing water barrels. That's when he realised that cylindrical objects were the hardest to suck into the vortex and he quickly clung on to one.

I haven't encountered an actual whirlpool, but I've had many small ones disrupt the peace in my heart. Questions with no answers that ran circles in my mind, tormenting me. Just as the seaman finds a barrel to save himself in the rough seas, I keep myself afloat with stories. Books may not solve all my problems, but at least they prevent me from sinking into the abyss.

Some things never change. I've grown out of my school days, but I still love thinking about books and stories, hugging them close, especially on a bad day. You may wonder if I would've become indifferent to most stories by now, but no way. I love reading more than ever, and I can already see myself spending my twilight years surrounded by books.

I hope this book will help you discover the joy of reading, the thrill of coming across a quote that resonates, the satisfaction of having found ten minutes in a busy day to sit down and read, the fun bookish discussions with friends, the excitement of finding a fictional soulmate, the reflective moments of introspection … I'm glad to have experienced them all. Dear reader, may this book journey onward with you.

Writing from my room, Winter 2017
Hwang Bo-reum

1

Read Bestsellers

Whenever someone approaches me for a book recommendation, I'll start by asking them several questions: What's your favourite book? What was the last book you read? Did you like it? How many books do you read a month? Do you prefer novels or essays? Who is your favourite author?

Without any idea of the individual's tastes, it's hard to offer them a good recommendation. I'm happy to share a title I've enjoyed, but all too often, my friends will buy a book I've gushed about only to never read it. These days, I no longer default to my personal favourites. But if someone struggles to answer my questions, I ask them: How about a bestseller?

Bestsellers, of course, have popular appeal. They may differ in their themes, depth, mood, or even strength of the writing, but what they have in common is how they resonate with the masses. That makes them an excellent place to start. (Of course, some bestsellers aren't the easiest reads – think Michael J. Sandel's *Justice: What's the Right Thing to Do?* – but these are exceptions.)

In 2015 and 2016, one of the top-selling books in South Korea was *The Courage to Be Disliked* by Ichiro Kishimi and Fumitake Koga, which follows the conversations between a philosopher and a young man frustrated with life.

The book, a blend of psychology and philosophy, references the theories of world-renowned psychiatrist Alfred Adler, but the dialogue format makes it easy to follow. I felt as if the book was telling me: *Be independent, free, and live a happy life. All you need is a little courage.*

We spend so much of our lives regretting the past and worrying about the future. One of my favourite quotes in the book is a timely reminder to live in the present moment:

> Then, let's dance in earnest the moments of the here and now … one has no use for destinations. As long as you are dancing, you will get somewhere.[1]

Sometimes I like to imagine what it'd be like to gather all those who've read the same book. For *The Courage to Be Disliked*, I see a vivid image of everyone dancing freely, enjoying life to the fullest.

If you want to get back into reading but don't know where to start, why not pick up a bestseller? Choose something that resonates with you, or one that is about a topic you're interested in. It makes you extra motivated to read whenever you have some free time. As your reading preferences start to take shape, that's when you'll go beyond bestsellers and start exploring the other shelves in the bookshop.

2

Read Beyond Bestsellers

Our family home had a bookcase that was so tall even my dad couldn't reach the topmost shelf. By the time I was in Grade 6, I was able to read almost any book I wanted. After school, I'd choose one at random, sit on the floor and start reading. If I found myself reading a couple of pages and thinking, *I could probably get into this one*, I'd take it back to my room.

Most of the books on the shelves belonged to my parents, some of which they bought when they were dating. The rest were my sister's, who was two years older than me. Sometimes I'd pick a book of my dad's, or one that my sister recommended. What I read those days was heavily influenced by them.

It was only in university that I started to develop my own tastes. With the money I earned from my part-time job, I stood in front of the shelves: this time, in a bookshop. I was spoilt for choice. One book at a time, I started to build my own bedside stack, which has since expanded into a sizeable collection.

I read somewhere that we tend to value more the things we've worked hard for. A paper aeroplane I made may not look any different from my friend's, but because I made it myself, I take pride in the fact that it's *mine*. And similarly, books I took the time and effort to select felt like *my books*.

The process of buying books can be a bit hit-and-miss. I've had my fair share of misses. Books that I thought had an interesting premise but lacked any depth whatsoever. Sometimes I'd get so worked up over the author's views – *Why does this book even exist!* – and slam it shut. But through such experiences, I've come to cultivate a discerning eye for good reads.

I look at two things: the contents page and the introduction. The former gives me a sense of the breadth and depth of the book, and from the latter I get a better understanding of the author's motivations for writing the book, as well as their style. If I find myself nodding along at the introduction, I'll read a couple of pages from the start and skim through a few more in the middle to get the overall vibe.

Ultimately, I listen to my feelings. It's the most straightforward approach. Sometimes I will buy a book after stumbling upon a quote that resonates with me, because if the author can capture my attention in just a few lines, it's almost certain I'll enjoy their work. Again, it's all about how the book makes me feel.

That was how I discovered *The Way of the World* by Nicolas Bouvier. I'd never heard of the author previously, but as I read the foreword, I marvelled at the unique lens with which he views the world. I was enthralled by his passion and curiosity for the places he has travelled to – Yugoslavia, Turkey, Iran, Pakistan, Afghanistan. I didn't need to check with my friends whether any of them had read the book; the book had my attention from the get-go. Immediately, I knew I wanted to read it. Here's one of my favourite lines:

> Confusion and loneliness are things the Serbs recognise … they immediately come forward with a bottle, a few shrivelled pears, and their kindly presence.[1]

What a lovely observation. Bouvier must be someone who pays careful attention to people and the world. I smile, certain that I'll enjoy the read. And with every chance discovery, I draw closer to books.

3

Read on the Train

Getting a job. That was basically what my early twenties after graduation was all about. At university, I busied myself trying to improve my GPA*, studying for the TOEIC exam†, writing covering letters to prospective employers, and preparing for interviews, only to fail them and wallow in disappointment. After a long struggle, I finally found a job. The company I joined was diversifying into the lucrative mobile phone industry and needed young, enthusiastic hires. I was – fortunately – one of the chosen ones.

I was determined to give 100 per cent at my first job, but soon I was overwhelmed by fatigue and stress. Maybe I had been so focused on getting the job that I'd never once paused to consider what life as a working adult

* Grade point average, the average mark for all of a student's courses.

† The Test of English for International Communication, an English proficiency test.

might look like. The absurdity and injustice of day-to-day office life was both surprising and enraging.

At the beginning, I was thrilled to land a job, and at a major conglomerate, no less. I was also grateful to work with great colleagues. But working overtime for several months wore me thin. I was staying in the office after midnight way too often, sometimes even when there wasn't any urgent work to be done – I was only staying because leaving before my bosses would make me look bad. Like a worker ant, I obeyed orders without question. I was a puppet that couldn't move without someone else pulling the strings. The lethargy seeped into my bones.

I stopped having a life outside of work, and the office became my whole world. I got a rude shock when I realised that I was becoming more at home at my work desk than my actual home. One morning, on the subway to work, I looked out the window at the inside of the dark tunnel, and thought, *If only I could get hospitalised for a week.*

There is a villain in Greek mythology called Procrustes. This innkeeper would invite in passing travellers and torture them in all sorts of cruel ways so that they would fit into his iron bed, either by stretching them until they died if they were too short, or amputating their legs if they were too tall.

For the next few years, life was a struggle. Going to work in the morning felt like being forced onto the iron bed, and I staggered home every night thoroughly spent. My body might be intact, but my soul was maimed.

Thinking back, it was during that dark period that reading, which until then was more of a hobby, played a more significant role in my life. I spent my commute time reading more desperately than ever. With my life reduced to a cog in the wheel, the rare moments I had to myself became even more precious. Instead of spacing out in dark tunnels, I turned my attention to books, hoping they would heal my damaged soul and my empty heart.

I don't remember exactly what I read back then, but I remember falling in love with essay collections. How could our thoughts be so similar despite living completely different lives, and so different when in the same circumstances? Reading essays taught me that life isn't about how high I climb; it's the stories, the experiences that make all the difference.

It was around that time that I read Ryu Shiva's *The Earth Traveller*. I am not religious, nor do I have the courage to travel as far as India, but his witty insights had me devouring it cover to cover and returning to Chapter 1 once more. In it, Shiva details a trip to India that he wanted to take, but which would force him to give up on other plans. He does not regret it and says the following:

But those were roads I didn't need to take, not in this life. Some roads are better left for my next life.[1]

As the subway train sped towards the next station, I mulled over whether I was heading down the 'roads I didn't need to take'. By just cracking open a book spine, our lives have now shifted a fraction away from those roads.

4

Read Small Books

The other day, my friends and I met at a café near Hongik University Station. We had bonded through a shared love for travel and writing, and decided to work on a Tokyo travelogue together. On this day, we were workshopping our essays when the last member arrived late from work. The moment she sat down, she reached for her bag.

She took out one book, a second one, a third and more, as if her bag housed a mysterious library within. The rest of us paused our conversation and fixed our gazes on the growing pile. There was a murmur of excitement.

'Wow, so pretty.'

'How unique.'

'What a charming cover.'

'The Japanese make such gorgeous books, don't they?'

The friend, who worked at a publishing house, said she thought the books might give us some inspiration. The

Japanese illustrated novels were smaller than a typical paperback novel, and slimmer, too. A friend picked one up, held it in their hand and exclaimed, 'Wow. I'd learn Japanese just to read this!'

Everyone at the table nodded in agreement. We were charmed.

Small books seem to be in fashion. Just the other day, I came across a palm-sized one that was only ninety-nine pages long. On the cover was the tagline '#1 *New York Times* Bestseller!'

There's a slim book sitting on my desk now, just 1 cm wider and 3 cm longer than the *NYT* bestseller. At 168 pages, it's slightly thicker, but because it's illustrated and the prose is only printed on one side of each page, it might be even shorter than the *NYT* bestseller. I love short reads – it'll only take an hour or two before I can bask in the satisfaction of having finished a book!

Small books have become my go-to whenever my mind is cluttered or when I'm having a bad day. The one on my table right now – *Um, Excuse Me* by Lee Kijun – has me laughing out loud. Give Lee any personality test and he will surely be at the extreme right on the 'how shy are you?' scale. Anyone who thinks of themselves as a shy, timid person needs to read this – they'll be delighted to discover, *Hey, I'm not as reserved as I thought!*

I nodded vigorously when I was reading the following section:

We all have days where we want to shake up our routine. Like a Bach-lover wanting to groove to a Beastie Boys song, a sudden urge to experience something new. We go searching, not knowing what we might find. Sometimes we return empty-handed, sometimes having gained so much more. And when we do, our horizons widen.[1]

Whenever I crave new experiences, I read. I travel about once a year, but I'm not the adventurous type. That's why I'm drawn to travel writing. For a timid person like me, it's the safest way to broaden my horizons.

5

Read Big Books

Last year, my friends and I had a simple year-end gathering. The most extroverted person among us suggested that we do a gift exchange with a twist. 'Let's each bring something from home that we don't use, but that's still good to be given as a present.'

For an entire week, I mulled over what to bring. Something in good condition and makes for a meaningful gift? I could only think of one thing: books.

Then came the harder question, which one? Because we planned to do a random draw, I had no idea who would get my present and what the person might enjoy. Thinking that I'd better avoid something overly niche, I ended up picking a 600-page art history book. It'd be interesting, I was sure, but then again, it was 600 pages. All my friends had busy careers. Would they find the gift ridiculous? Or worse, think that I was ridiculous? Who would have the time for a thick book like that?

On the day of the gathering, I was super anxious. Was I being too self-centred by choosing something only I would like? I quickly stuffed a few paperbacks into my already bulging bag, and only then did the anxiety ebb a little. When the last friend arrived at 10 p.m. after work, looking absolutely beaten, I was relieved that I had brought backup gifts. The 600-page book could now be the 'extra option', and if no one was enthusiastic, I'd take it back home.

Finally, it was time to reveal the presents. I took out the paperbacks first, before plonking the heavy book on the table. But guess what? I had fretted for days for nothing. Everyone exclaimed in delight at the art history book, and the paperbacks lay forgotten. The friend who eventually brought it home was pleased as punch, quipping that carrying it already made her feel scholarly.

A few days later, I was on the phone with a friend, and we spent close to an hour discussing why I had worried so much about how the others would view the book and me, and the fact that everyone turned out to be surprisingly receptive.

'It's the thirst,' my friend said sagely.

'Thirst?' I echoed.

'Yeah, the thirst for knowledge. Don't we love a good challenge?'

I nodded vigorously – not that my friend could see – and replied, 'You're right.'

The thicker the book, the stronger our desire to conquer it. Even if the pages seem never-ending, and despite starting to forget what I had read, knowing that a wealth of knowledge remains to be discovered keeps me going. There's no bigger satisfaction than getting up to stretch after finishing a thick book, as though I've conquered a steep mountain, and eager for an even bigger challenge.

Just the other day, I finished Yuval Noah Harari's *Sapiens: A Brief History of Humankind*. It was a breathtaking hike; I thoroughly enjoyed every moment. The book overturns our common sense and argues that societal progress doesn't make us happier. Instead, the author claims that the hunter-gatherers were much happier than the farmers after the First Agricultural Revolution. He follows with a rhetorical question: if advancement in civilisation doesn't guarantee individual happiness, then what should be the way forward?

But no matter how amazing a book is, even if reading it will be a life-changing experience, thickness is always a deterrent. When I'm reading thick books, I remind myself not to calculate how long it'll take me. Instead, I focus on small progress goals, such as reading for thirty minutes, or an hour. Once I hit the goal, I close the book. I did read the last few chapters of *Sapiens* over a weekend, but for two thirds of the book I had worked through it steadily, an hour a day.

6

Underlining and Annotations

We are never 'just reading'. When I'm reading, I'm doing multiple things at once. I am reflecting on my past mistakes at the same time I'm learning about the future of AI and technology. In the process, I'm also discovering more of the world and myself. But here's the awkward thing. When I close the book, and sometimes from that very moment, I forget everything I've learnt.

I think this is why some people claim that reading is 'useless'. How many of us can remember a book we read last week, not to mention a year ago? I'd struggle to even recall the title, as if my memory is shrouded by thick fog. *Is reading really a waste of time?* The thought fills me with dread.

Until I can find a way to save everything in my memory, I'll settle for collecting my favourite quotes. I may not remember everything, but at the very least I want to make sure that I won't lose the good sentences. That's why I always have a pencil when I read, so that I can underline the sentences that speak to me. Occasionally, I scribble a note at the side. Whenever I need to refresh my memory, I can simply follow the trail of pencil markings.

Because I'm so used to doing that, it feels weird to read without a pencil. I always keep an extra or two in my bags, and on the rare occasion I am without one, I won't (can't) read.

But underlining the text doesn't solve the issue of the 'forgetting curve'. Some time back, I was reading the Korean edition of Alain de Botton's *The Consolations of Philosophy*. I liked it, yet I couldn't help but think – *He's really milking this, isn't he? Hasn't he already written something else about Socrates, Seneca and Schopenhauer?* But then I thought, *that isn't a flaw*, so I cast aside my complaints and returned to the text.

After finishing the book, I put it back onto the shelf and soon forgot about it. One day, a sudden thought struck me, and I quickly pulled out a book from my bookcase titled, in Korean, *The Happiness of Young Werther*. I zoomed in on the contents page and confirmed my suspicions – it was the exact same book as *The Consolations of Philosophy*. I had read *Consolations* without realising that it was a new edition that opted for a more faithful title to the English, and I had annotated it as though I was reading it for the first time!

I snorted in disbelief. Then a thought tickled my brain. Haven't I read about that in a story before? I pulled out Patrick Süskind's *Three Stories and a Reflection*, which, true to its title, consists of three short stories and a personal essay. There it was. In the last story, 'Amnesia in Litteris', he describes how, despite reading voraciously for more than three decades, he barely remembers the details of any book. I had just experienced the same 'literary memory loss'. Süskind says: 'If we don't even retain a shadow of memory, despite having read it only recently, then why do we read?'[1] He mulls the question over and arrives at the conclusion that reading isn't about *remembrance* but the *change* that can come from reading a book.

You can transform your life – Süskind believes this is why we read. I repeat this under my breath, feeling comforted knowing that if I am a slightly different person after reading a book, it's OK if I don't remember every word.

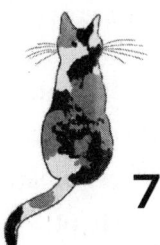

7

Always Have a Book With You

I read somewhere that authors are voracious readers. I would imagine so. When I read, I also feel the urge to create something of my own. Likewise, I don't think I've ever come across a writer who doesn't read. Come to think of it, reading and writing are one and the same.

Off the top of my head, I can already think of three similarities. First, unlike TV or video games, you don't get instant gratification. That's why you rarely hear of people who get into writing or reading overnight. It takes time. The more we do it, the deeper the joy. Such happiness isn't a passing shower, but a steady drizzle.

Second, many people talk about wanting to write or read, but not many actually do it. In *Wild Mind: Living the Writer's Life*, writer and Zen practitioner Natalie Goldberg talks about how most people spend their entire lives circling around the idea of wanting to write but the difficulty puts them off. And her advice is: just do it.

The same applies to reading. Instead of stopping at the thought, turn it into action. *Do it.*

Third, you can read or write anywhere. Of course, some places are more conducive than others, but technically, anywhere is possible. That solves the problem in the second point. All you need is a book. And if you're writing, a notepad and pen. Even the memo app on your phone will work.

Bring a book and notepad everywhere with you. That way, you can read and write anytime, whenever you are bored or waiting for someone. It takes a while for the habit to settle in, but one day you'll find yourself feeling oddly unsettled without them.

Having a smartphone and a book with me all the time means I can write and read whenever I want. I like to bring a page-turner out because it keeps me glancing at my bag every now and then, and that makes me extra motivated to read whenever I have a moment. One such book is *The Unsocial Sociability* by Japanese philosopher Yoshimichi Nakajima.

Nakajima criticises the unique collectivism of Japanese society. In *The Unsocial Sociability*, Nakajima references Immanuel Kant's theories to explore how to extract oneself from societal dependence yet not be completely isolated. The book title itself is a nod to Kant's theory that it is in human nature to form social connections yet strive for individualism. To those struggling to form social connections, Nakajima has the following advice:

You just need one single bond … A person you can truly trust, a person that rejoices in your existence. If there's one such person in your life, you'll be able to keep going.[1]

Just for this moment, allow me to take the liberty to divide people into those who carry a book with them all the time, and those who don't. People who read, who open their eyes and ears to the words of others, and those who don't. I hope to always be in the former group. It's time to head out, and as usual, I'll be picking my companion for the day.

8

Choose Books, Not the Internet

I have a short attention span, but reading has always been an exception. I can melt into the prose for hours on end and automatically block out all ambient noise. It takes someone to practically shout into my ears before I look up with a start.

But out of nowhere, I found myself struggling to read. Each time I wanted to dive right into the story, my attention would drift. It took a while to even settle down and open a book, but in no time, I found myself getting distracted. I had lost the freedom to lose myself in books anytime, anywhere.

I almost always end up on my phone, even when no one's messaged me, and I have no notifications. I reach for it on reflex, and it will be another five or ten minutes before I look up with a jolt. Because I keep getting distracted, I'm reading extra slowly, and that in turn frustrates me further.

Reading turns into an intense wrestling match where I have to strategise how to maximise my attention span.

I start to approach reading in the same way I would a problem. It's a tight match, but because I am still tasting the victory of finishing a book – albeit a lot more slowly – I can't break out of the vicious cycle.

Why is it so hard to focus these days? Nicholas Carr, in *The Shallows: What the Internet Is Doing to Our Brains*, claims it's because of the internet. As we get used to instantaneous gratification, we lose our ability to focus.

Our brain's structure changes over the course of our life, especially when we do something repeatedly, both physically and mentally. Neural plasticity explains why we form habits, why we tend to make the same choice in the same situation, why one might crave chocolate specifically at three in the afternoon, and why we automatically turn on the TV at ten in the evening. In *The Shallows*, Carr references a quote from the French scientist Léon Dumont:

Flowing water hollows out a channel for itself which grows broader and deeper; and when it later flows again, it follows the path traced by itself before. Just so, the impressions of outer objects fashion for themselves more and more appropriate paths in the nervous system, and these vital paths recur under similar external stimulation, even if they have been interrupted for some time.[1]

Like flowing water, the more time we spend on the internet, the more it erodes our ability to focus. Not just that, but it also affects our analytical ability. Our brains become the very things that distract us from our tasks, luring us to pick up our phones instead.

Instead of forcing ourselves to read, we need to ask ourselves this: What's making it more difficult to read these days? There are always other fun activities competing for our time, but the internet is also a distraction. To draw closer to books, we have to distance ourselves from the internet. And according to Carr, to rewire our brains and improve our attention span, we should read. The more we read, the better we will be able to focus.

9

Use a Timer App

I read somewhere that one way to find happiness is by being focused and engaged in what we do. I would like to add that focus can enhance the joy of reading. No matter how interesting a book is, if you can't concentrate, you won't be able to enjoy it fully. That's why, these days, I've been trying to do something about my attention span.

One thing I had attempted (and quickly given up) was quitting the internet. Alex Rühle and Susan Maushart, in their respective books *No Signal: My Half-Year Offline*[1] and *The Winter of Our Disconnect,* talk about their experiences of going cold turkey for six months. Rühle, who embarked on the challenge alone in Germany, claims that he was better able to hear his inner voice without the distraction of the internet. Meanwhile, Maushart went off-grid with her teenage kids, and in those six months her children were visibly more engaged with their surroundings and even found new hobbies and dreams.

Yet, at the end of the six months, they returned to the world of the internet. It's simply impractical to cut internet use for the rest of our lives. When I read their books, what interested me wasn't so much their experience of going cold turkey, but the idea of restraint. How can I regulate my screen time so that I can spend more time on things I like, such as reading? A friend told me they would keep their phone turned off in the morning so that they could focus on important tasks. That's a good tip. I also have a friend who said they made do without a data plan for their phone. Sounds doable, too.

As for me, I constantly remind myself of my resolve. Once I start scrolling aimlessly, I tell myself to stop. I deleted the apps I used (too) frequently from my home screen, namely Naver and Daum, the two major web portals in Korea, and the only social media app on my phone – Facebook. Adding the few extra steps to access the apps works reasonably well as a deterrent without going to the extent of deleting them entirely.

But doing that alone doesn't help to improve my concentration. I like to use a timer app when I read. Mine has a simple interface – just the time, down to the second. I set the timer, usually for twenty minutes, and unless there's a life-threatening emergency or if my lovely nephew wants to play, I put everything aside and immerse myself fully in the book.

When the timer rings, I take a quick break before doing another twenty minutes. Three rounds make an hour and it's as if my engine has revved up. I no longer need the timer that day to continue reading.

10

Read Classics

The other day, I was talking to a friend who had just finished reading Hermann Hesse's *Demian*.

'I think authors who come after Hesse's time are incredible,' she said.

'Oh, why so?' I asked.

'After reading this masterpiece, how can anyone think of writing their own book? *Demian* already tells us everything about life!'

Talk about being a fan. I first read *Demian* many years ago, but when I turned thirty sometime back, I decided to reread it. I loved it even more, so that I went around urging everyone to read it.

Italo Calvino, in his book *Why Read the Classics?*, says this:

The classics are those books about which you usually hear people saying: 'I'm rereading ...', never 'I'm reading ...'.[1]

Why, though? Calvino says it's 'an act of hypocrisy on the part of people ashamed to admit they have not read a famous book'. I mean, I'm not completely innocent in this regard, but I swear I did read *Demian* before, and for the longest time I thought he was the main protagonist (it's actually Sinclair). Despite reading it for the second time, I remained as impressed by Hesse's writing.

Honestly, I don't feel embarrassed at not having read many classics. Who can claim they've read everything anyway? That said, hopefully I'll be able to discover another enduring work that will resonate with me as much.

In his book, Calvino argues that the classics 'help us understand who we are, and the point we have reached'. Great as they might be, I can't imagine reading classics exclusively, and if there's someone out there who does, they have my respect.

Let's say I've just finished Samuel Beckett's *Waiting for Godot*. It'd probably take me at least a week, or even two to fully digest the story. For the next few years, I occasionally think of Vladimir and Estragon, and how, in a parallel world somewhere, they're still spending their lives waiting for Godot. And one day, I realise suddenly that I'm no different. I am also barely making it through each day, waiting for something that I can't quite articulate. For the rest of my life, the characters remain etched in my mind.

With books that exert such a powerful influence on my life, I have neither the confidence nor the ability to read them in succession. I need some time and space with my reflections. In the meantime, I have to switch to a different genre, and only when I'm ready again will I be able to reach for something like *A Room of One's Own* or *One Day in the Life of Ivan Denisovich*.

Calvino doesn't encourage us to read only classics. In fact, he says that to get the most out of classics, we need to read contemporary works because the latter provide a layered perspective that helps contextualise and enrich our reading experience of the classics.

To read only classics carries the risk of being stuck in the time-space of the past and losing our way in the present. Likewise, reading only contemporary works may trap us in a superficial outlook on life. As always, balance is important.

I'll leave you with my favourite quote from *Why Read the Classics?* Because no matter what you think of classics, you can't deny this: 'reading the classics is always better than not reading them'.

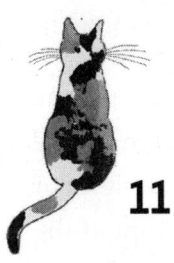

11

Read Novels

'Why read fiction when everything's fake?'

Life is busy – why care about people who don't even exist? If you are so free, why not spend the time on yourself? Whenever I get questions like these, I firmly tell the person that they've got it wrong. Those of us who read fiction care very much about our lives, thank you very much.

When I read novels, it's as if I'm looking at my own life through the fictional characters. Our lives may be vastly different, but I see some parts of myself in their actions and words. That's why a good novel is unputdownable.

Novels don't tell us 'how to live' but show us that 'it's possible to live in a different way'. It's easy to get stuck in our narrow perspective on life and put pressure on ourselves. What we see or hear becomes the limits of our horizons. We become afraid of stepping outside our comfort zone, living each day treading on thin ice. Ironically, the closer we get towards our goals, the more cautious and fearful we become. But when things don't unfold according to our expectations, our shoulders slump in despair. Because we have no idea how to get out of the doldrums, we sink deeper into misery.

But when a person with a narrow outlook on what life looks like starts to read, they change. The moment we realise that the life we struggle to flee from might be what someone else yearns for, our worldview, once the size of a keyhole, expands as if we're standing in front of a full-length window, and our ears, clogged with lies and exaggeration, clear to welcome genuine voices speaking to us. We're still living the same life as yesterday, but with our eyes and ears open; we become a different person. Knowing that there isn't only one path in life assuages our worries, and instead of pacing nervously at every crossroad, we gain the courage to walk ahead with confidence.

Something I love about novels is that despite knowing that I'll never get answers, I'm free to ask the questions. No one knows for sure why a character behaves in a certain way. In that sense, every interpretation is the right answer, or maybe there are only wrong answers. That keeps us thinking. Doesn't that mirror life itself?

If ever there is a list of the most inscrutable fictional characters, I bet Bartleby from the short story 'Bartleby, the Scrivener' by Herman Melville would be one of them.

It's impossible to know what he's thinking when he says his famous line: 'I would prefer not to.'

'Will you tell me, Bartleby, where you were born?'
'I would prefer not to.'
'Will you tell me anything about yourself?'
'I would prefer not to.'[1]

What a gentle rebuff with no ill intention, no disrespect. One can't help but wonder what makes him drop all his duties suddenly and spend his time staring at a brick wall? Why is he refusing to budge when asked to leave the office? Perhaps even Melville himself doesn't know. And so, we keep questioning. What is Bartleby thinking about? Or come to think of it, do we even know what's on our own mind? Why is it that the important things in life have no answers? Is it OK not to know what we're doing? Is that what life is like? Novels taught me that we can only keep searching for answers, and no, they are never just 'someone else's story'.

12

Read Poetry

Several years ago, my friend gave me a poetry collection. I still remember the date – 12 January 2013. On the first page he wrote: *Let's keep writing, always.* My friend had wanted to become a poet. He studied poetry and regularly organised poetry readings with well-known poets. 'Occasionally, I see people reading on the subway, but it's never poetry,' he quipped with a laugh.

'Why do you like poetry?'

I must have asked him the question more than once. Poetry is difficult, at least to me. I don't get the appeal.

His reply was straightforward. He told me he loved it, especially when he was mulling over a particular word or imagery the poet had chosen.

'Imagine a line in a poem that goes: *That day, I smelt the sun.* Doesn't make sense, right? How can we smell the sun? Yet the poet says that. It's stuck in my head and whenever I see the sun, it's as if I can almost smell it.

As I'm walking down the street on a bright sunny day, I can't help but wonder what or who the poet was thinking about when they wrote it.'

OK, but this is exactly why I find poetry difficult. Often I tilt my head in confusion. *Why did the poet use this particular word?* The unconventional use of language, especially common in contemporary poetry, frustrates me. I have no idea what it's trying to convey.

But I have another friend who loves poetry precisely because of its ambiguity. Because there isn't a fixed answer, every reader has the freedom to decide. If the poem stirs something in you, don't keep questioning it, she tells me. Simply allow yourself to *feel*. Isn't that what reading poetry is about? What a fresh perspective. I've never paused to consider that it's the ambiguity that frees the readers.

Of course, there are also poets who adhere to a strict poetry structure. And in *I Love Writing Poems*, a collection of essays by twelve Korean poets, poet Hwang In-chan says the following:

A single poem holds little meaning. To be truly meaningful and complete, one needs a collection or several poems.[1]

Hwang was writing from the perspective of writing poetry, but I think the same applies to reading poetry.

Can we really say that we understand a poem if we have only read a single work by the poet?

In *I'm Fading Away Each Time We Fight*,[2] the author Eun Yoo says that the harder life gets, the more we crave poetry. According to Eun, poetry doesn't comfort or heal. Quoting poet Hwang Dong-kyu, Eun claims that poetry trains us to become used to a life that isn't always happy. Through poetry, we learn to find contentment in our misery.

Recently, the friend who'd given me the poetry collection stopped talking about wanting to be a poet. He hasn't given up on writing poetry, nor did he suddenly lose interest. He still enjoys it, but there are also other things that he has grown to enjoy as much. The other day, I asked him, 'Why do you think people read poetry?'

'Because we're hurting on the inside, and poetry shares the pain with us.'

That day when I got home, I dug out the book he'd given me in 2013 – Kim Seung-hee's *Hope is Lonely*. I opened it to a random page.

The poem 'What it Means to "Pay No Heed"' starts like this:

In the end, don't you think all poems share the same
Precariousness of Existence
Lee Sang
Kim Yoojung, Kafka

Their words
teeter on the edge of life[3]

It makes me wonder. If we're reading poetry at bedtime, does that mean we've been living in uncertainty the entire day? Are we hoping to find camaraderie?

13

Online Bookshops, Facebook, Instagram

I'm always on the lookout to see what people are reading, or searching for a book that was quoted by someone in an interview or on a talk show, and of course, to be up to date with the latest buzz reads. There are so many books I want to read, but that doesn't stop me from adding more.

Honestly, I'm starting to panic. *Can I ever finish reading everything?* But instead of fretting, there's only one thing to do: focus on the book in my hands. Sometimes, for an extra dose of motivation, I place my next read in a prominent position, where I can see it all the time.

Even when I'm reading, I'm pausing now and then to look up more books. Whenever I see references to other books, I feel as though the author is giving me a personal recommendation. In the same way academia tracks how many times a book is cited, a book that has been referenced in a book (or multiple books) somehow feels more trustworthy. And if it's a topic that I'm already interested in, I immediately add it to my shopping cart. My shopping cart functions as my TBR list, and I check out a few each time I am in the mood for book shopping.

I also follow book news closely on Facebook. My feed is full of posts from publishers, bricks-and-mortar bookshops, literary podcasts, indie bookshops and news sites, so I get almost real-time updates on new releases or books that are making the rounds on the internet. And whenever I see my friends post about a book they've read recently, I make a mental note. Despite hearing some of these titles for the first time, I eagerly add them to my shopping cart.

One of the books that I got to know through Facebook was *For Pain to Be a Path* by Kim Seung-seop, a scholar on social dynamics. I came across a review of it, and later, a friend posted about it. My curiosity was piqued. I went to search it up, and the following line in the author's bio caught my attention: *Society should be held responsible if the average person lacks a sense of pride in life.* Intrigued, I clicked into the book sample and read the introduction. According to Kim, having a robust healthcare system alone isn't enough; society should take care of the health of every individual. Immediately, I knew this was a book that I wanted to read, and it was as though I'd been waiting for it all this while.

Besides getting book news from Facebook, I like to go on Instagram. It's amazing how people put up aesthetic photos of books they've read in the same way they post pictures of their travels. I can see what others have been reading by scrolling through tags like #bookstagram #bookrecommendations #bookstack. Each tag has millions of posts, and more are being posted as we speak.

Gorgeous flat lays, sometimes with a can of beer, a cup of coffee, or close-up shots of quotes … It's impossible to stop scrolling. There are so many books that I'm seeing for the first time. My shopping cart is ready!

14

Bed, Night and Lights

When I'm going on holiday, I always pack a couple of books in my luggage. I do it without fail, despite knowing that I'm not going to follow through my plans of sitting somewhere, soaking in the local vibes and reading leisurely. When I went for a nine-day trip to the Czech Republic, Hungary and Austria, I brought along five books, including the Korean editions of *Éloge de la marche* by David Le Breton, *Like Water for Chocolate* by Laura Esquivel and *Die Glut* by Sándor Márai.

I imagine myself relaxing with a book, just like in a scene from a movie or poster. A beautiful woman reading – was it *Do You Like Brahms?* – under a parasol at the beach in Bali, or a middle-aged man sitting in an alleyway café near the Eiffel Tower, propping *Identity* by Milan Kundera on his lap and nursing a cup of coffee as he reads. I imagine him reading over his spectacles; the image feels incomplete otherwise.

How romantic. A person deep in concentration on a book exudes a special energy. A vibe. A certain look in their eyes. As if quiet, intimate changes are blooming in them, and I find that so beautiful. I want to experience that for myself.

But each time I'm on a holiday, I never end up staying in a single spot for long. I sit down at a café, but less than thirty minutes later I get restless. I stuff the book in my bag and go exploring again, even if it's just walking down the street. It's great that I'm soaking in the local vibes, but at the same time, I get a little upset at myself.

I guess I'll need at least a month or two in Europe for the sights of Prague, Budapest and Vienna to feel like everyday life. Only then will I be able to settle down into a routine and read at a café. But on a short, nine-day holiday, my attention drifts to everything else except the book in my hands.

Or maybe I'm just romanticising this whole thing. I should stop wallowing in my 'failure'. But that doesn't mean I'm going to give up. Instead of trying to fit myself into a stereotypical image, I'm going to find beauty in my everyday life.

And I do. In my bedroom, at night, accompanied by the warm glow of the bedside lamp. Forget the expensive air ticket, all it cost was a 70,000-won light. In the evening, I wait for the sun to set and, when the sky darkens, I switch on the light. I settle snugly in bed, sinking into my pillows as I flip open a book. Right in my own room, I've found the romantic moment I was looking for. I've become one with the prose.

I'm now reading Jung Hyeyoon's *Bed and Books*. Isn't that such a romantic title? Every night, I spend some time in its pages, and in that time, I set aside all my responsibilities, societal expectations, and fully embrace my inner romantic. Under the warm glow of the lamp, I smile and turn the page.

> Whether it's fatigue, anxiety, worry, anticipation, or anything else, tomorrow, as always, I'm going to replace them all with a book.[1]

Lying in bed with a book and the glow from the bedside lamp, I feel as though I could travel anywhere – any country, city, town, or café. Every night, I get to enjoy my romantic moment. Perhaps I've become an inspiration for someone else, just like the woman in Bali and the middle-aged man in Paris were for me, but in this moment, what's truly important isn't the vibes, but the fact that I'm reading.

15

Favourite Author

My friend and I met as colleagues, but we behaved like desk mates in high school, squabbling over the most random things and shadowing each other all the time. Our vibes matched well, and when our gazes met, we would wiggle our eyebrows and give each other the *Hey, make me laugh* look. Throughout the time we were working together, we shared tons of jokes and laughter.

What I admired most about her, among many things, is how she has one favourite author, and she only reads his work. Whether it's before bed, when she's bored, or when she's feeling down, it's always Murakami, and only Murakami. I'm amazed at her single-mindedness, and it makes me feel as though I'm missing out on something if I don't read Murakami. Not that I haven't tried. *Kafka on the Shore, The Wind-up Bird Chronicle, Norwegian Wood...* The Murakami books I've attempted to read but ultimately gave up.

When I told her I could never finish a Murakami book, she urged me to try *Dance, Dance, Dance*. Not wanting to disappoint her, I persevered, and for the first time in my life read a Murakami novel from cover to cover. Perhaps she found my efforts endearing; that year, for my birthday, she gave me a Murakami essay collection – *Murakami Radio*. And feeling once again that I shouldn't disappoint her, I finished it. That was how I ended up being a fan of Murakami (just his essays, though). Once, I texted her: *What is it about Murakami that you like so much?*

And she replied: *His honesty, the way he puts across raw emotions, the clarity in his prose, the quiet strength, and his unparalleled imagination! And of course, not forgetting his humour. Perhaps you can even call that love...**

According to Bertrand Russell, a 'friendly interest' in things and people is the secret to a happy life. I guess nothing makes my friend happier than Murakami putting out a new book. It makes me think that it's a blessing to be an ardent fan of someone.

Indeed, being a fan of an author adds to the fun of reading. In the past, what had mattered to me was only whether the book was interesting or not. But when I started to pay attention to the title and who wrote it, it felt as if I'd stepped into a whole new wondrous world where authors and readers are connected by stories.

* Actual text received in 2006.

I imagine that somewhere, in a small room, an author pores over their manuscript for several months or even years. And elsewhere, a reader snuggles in bed with a book every night, praying that life can be kinder. Their connection begins at the shelves in the bookshop, and in the time that they spent in each other's company, the fictional world that the author creates breathes hope into the reader's real life. And the reader is likewise generous with her praise – *What a wonderful book. I really like your stories. Maybe you can even call that love …*

Unlike my friend, I can't dedicate myself to reading only one author. I have several favourites, and one of them is Paul Auster. I read *The Brooklyn Follies* because I was intrigued by the title, and I ended up devouring *Moon Palace* and *Leviathan* one after the other and became a huge fan. I've also read *The New York Trilogy*, *Sunset Park* and *Hand to Mouth*, as well as his recent works.

The Brooklyn Follies remains my favourite, maybe because it was where it all started. I even developed a soft spot for Brooklyn, a place I've never even been!

It's as if the book is telling me this: *Even though I'm a lonely soul, thank you for reaching for my hand and giving me fresh hope.* I feel comforted that I don't have to be too disappointed even if things didn't turn out the way I wanted, and that even if I'm standing at the edge of despair, I'm still lucky to have a friend that I can laugh and crack jokes with.

I was looking for a quiet place to die.[1]

Despite its bleak opening line, the book never loses its sense of hope, and that's why I ended up falling for this book. And Paul Auster.

16

Books and Drinks

Have you noticed a common trait of passionate people? They put in extra effort to enjoy something that they already love in the first place. Like how they might relax with a hot shower before snuggling on the couch with their favourite drama, alongside a perfectly chilled can of beer and a savoury snack. Or the cinephile who searches for reviews and essays the moment they leave the theatre, eager to know what others are saying about the movie.

Same with an art hobbyist who puts on a small exhibition with their friends from the painting club, their passion further fuelled by the new challenge. What about a baseball fan? Maybe they'll cajole their family to watch a game together and, on that day, everyone comes in the team shirt, waving their banners in excitement.

Masayuki Kusumi, whose work *Kodoku no Gurume* was adapted into popular Japanese drama series *Solitary Gourmet*, wrote an essay titled 'Daytime Bathhouse and

Drinking' about a man who, after mulling over how to maximise the pleasure of drinking beer, starts to visit the bathhouse regularly. He spends an hour or two soaking in the hot tubs at the bathhouse before stopping by his regular drinking hole for an ice-cold beer. I haven't been to the bathhouse in years, but I can't help but wonder how much more delicious the beer would taste.

Come to think of it, the book bar in Yeonhui-dong is my 'bathhouse'. The vibes are great, the drinks delicious. Surrounded by patrons reading intently at the next table or speaking in hushed tones so as not to disturb others, I find myself enjoying my book even more than usual.

I remember my first visit. Passing the entrance sign that read WE LOVE SOLO DINERS, the space opened up to the tables in the main dining area. A couple of customers were reading alone with a glass of wine. I put down my bag on the table, perused the menu and ordered a drink.

'One Cutty Sark highball, please.'

The owner-cum-bartender, also the author of the book *Time to Drink a Novel*, spoke.

'That's a non-sweet cocktail, is that OK?'

Smiling, I nodded. *I wanted to try this because I'd read about it in your book,* I added in my mind. I took out Paul Harding's *Enon* and started to read. Music was playing in the background, and the only white noise was the occasional clink of ice cubes as the bartender made the drinks, and the rustle of paper. Everyone was deep in concentration on their books. The atmosphere was even better than I had expected.

I sank deep into the chair, sipping my zesty drink as I turned the pages. This must be how drinking beer after a hot soak feels like. Come to think of it, there are so many more ways to add joy to what I love. I looked around. How did I not think of pairing a book with a drink?

When I left the bar two hours later, I basked in the contentment of having read several more chapters. A chilly evening wind blew. I was reminded of the last few lines in *Time to Drink a Novel*. Time to go home and read a little more before going to bed. What a perfect end to a great day.

The sky is darkening, but you don't want to go home yet. It's just one of those days. If you don't have plans and you aren't sure what do, how about reading a book?[1]

You Don't Always Have to Finish It

The one book that I've attempted to read multiple times only to give up again and again is Umberto Eco's *The Name of the Rose*. The long citations in the introduction were enough to put me off, not to mention the words in several languages left untranslated. My eyes simply glazed over the names of people, places and whatnot.

An older female friend – I call her Eonnie – had recommended me the book, and when I told her about giving up, she encouraged me to keep going. 'Just get past the first hundred pages and you won't be able to put it down.' Her words seemed to cast a spell on me and I would pick up the book over and over (only to give up several pages in).

But because everyone around me was raving about the book and the author, I refused to give up so easily. Finally, I got past the hundred-page mark, and just as Eonnie had said, the book was unputdownable. I grew so fond of the Franciscan friar William that for a while, he was my dream guy.

'Just get past the first hundred pages.'

The next time Eonnie said the same thing about a book, it was *Walden* by Henry David Thoreau. When she told me the book was about living in harmony with nature, I was intrigued, but the hundred-page hurdle proved to be a challenge. When I finally did it, Thoreau and his words took root in my mind, and I still find myself thinking about them every now and then.

Of course, there are also many books that I simply never return to. If I'm no longer curious about what happens next, I won't hesitate to close a book. No lingering regrets whatsoever. Books and people are the same. Just like how some individuals can connect with us more deeply than others, the same applies to books. Instead of trying to salvage a failing relationship, I'd be better off finding a book I can vibe with.

I know some people hate the idea of giving up midway. But by insisting on finishing a book you no longer want to read, you're taking time away from the books you're truly interested in. When reading is reduced to a dreaded chore, many people end up distancing themselves from books altogether.

Perseverance is great, but if you find your interest in a book waning, it might not be the right book for you at that point. That said, things change, and so do you, your interests and what you want to read. Who knows? It might be the perfect book next time.

Fate works in curious ways. A book that you had struggled to get into could end up becoming one of your all-time favourites. *Walden* was that book for me. Each time I reread it, I discover new quotes that I'd overlooked previously, making it a new experience all over again.

In 1845, Thoreau moved to the woods around Walden Pond in Concord, Massachusetts. There he built a cabin, and for the next two years and two months he lived in seclusion, distilling life to its essence. Reading about his life inspired me to think about how I could also escape from the rat race to truly live a life I wanted.

> I went to the woods because I wished to live deliberately, to front only the essential facts of life, and see if I could not learn what it had to teach, and not, when I came to die, discover that I had not lived. I did not wish to live what was not life, living is so dear; nor did I wish to practise resignation, unless it was quite necessary. I wanted to live deep and suck out all the marrow of life, to live so sturdily and Spartan-like as to put to rout all that was not life, to cut a broad swath and shave close, to drive life into a corner, and reduce it to its lowest terms ...[1]

I respect Thoreau for looking beyond the superficial things in life in search for his ideal way of living, and so I eagerly recommended his books to my friends.

'Sounds great, but that sounds almost like fantasy to me right now. I can't relate at all,' said a friend.

I replied, 'It's OK. Who knows? It might be the right book next time.'

18

Are Books Useful?

After a long day where my schedule was practically broken down by the minute, I finally got to lie down in bed with a book. Instead of dabbling in different hobbies, I devote all my free time to reading. Sometimes I wonder, *What do I hope to get out of this? What keeps me going?*

I like books, but is that the only reason? Do I not want to get something else out of it? Chinese philosopher Zhuangzi speaks of 'the usefulness of uselessness'. What seems to be useless can in fact be useful. I think it applies to reading, too. In fact, reading is quite useful.

In the heyday of literary appreciation, people aspired to be voracious readers, believing that a well-read person was a successful one. It's nice to have aspirations, but I baulk at linking the utility of books to success, or at least, I can't connect Shakespeare with the stereotypical definition of success. That makes me wonder if someone who has read Zhuangzi would still insist that reading a lot brings success? Even if they used to think this way, I'm sure that reading will open their eyes and minds to a bigger world beyond success and failure.

Back to the question: *So, what do I hope to get out of books?*

I hope to become stronger, to stand firm by my convictions, and to become a more mature person. Someone neither arrogant nor naïve. Someone who can be honest about my feelings, yet not let emotions overwhelm me. I want to keep learning and become wiser. I want to see the world, to better understand others.

Listing them like this makes me a little embarrassed. These are lofty aspirations, I know. Maybe it's easier to chase the conventional idea of success. But this is what keeps me reading. Because I'm lacking in many ways, I hope to fill myself with books.

A while ago, I watched *Things to Come* starring Isabelle Huppert. Imagine my shock to see everything I aspire to be reflected in a single character. Huppert brings Nathalie to life – a middle-aged woman who deals with her husband's betrayal and her mother's death with steely calm and grace. It's a powerful reminder that while we cannot control everything that happens, we can choose how we deal with these unexpected situations. In the movie, Nathalie holds a book in her hand. When life falls apart, when people betray my trust, books are also the constant in my life, accompanying me through the highs and lows. To me, the book in her hand symbolises not just knowledge, but her maturity and her ability to adapt to her circumstances.

Just as Michel de Montaigne writes in *Essays*:

We must learn to suffer whatever we cannot evade.[1]

As I underlined the sentence, a ripple of emotion spread in my heart. But at the same time, I couldn't help but doubt. Can I truly embody something so profound? Would I be able to do what he says?

Nathalie gives me hope that it's possible. What we read will distil into us, and one day, rise to give us the strength and support we need. When Nathalie says that she's OK and that she's handling things well, I can believe that it's genuine. One day, I'll be able to say, 'I'm fine,' and be truly fine. Books have taught me how to embrace all the good and bad in life. Reading may seem useless, but it's what makes us stronger.

19

Visiting the Library

I only started visiting the library a few years ago. I'm simply so used to buying books that I've never paused to consider that I could borrow them. One day, I chanced upon a library in my neighbourhood and, realising that it's only a seven-minute walk from my home, I started going more often and I'm now a loyal patron.

It's a small but cosy library. In the centre are two huge tables lined with chairs. They're empty most of the time, save for a patron or two quietly reading. However, when the school holidays start, a throng of kids play in the children's section, and some sit around the tables to read manhwa (comics) or play games on their smartphones.

In the past two or three years, I've also noticed a spike in patrons coming during summer to enjoy the free air-conditioning. But because I prefer to read in the comfort of my home, I don't usually stay long.

A sense of contentment spreads within me as I browse the shelves. If I want to, I can read every single book here! Whether it's the books I've been meaning to get to, books I'm seeing for the first time, those with worn covers or brand-new ones with stiff spines – every book seems to be waving at me: *Come, read me!* I can take my own sweet time to browse, and even if the books I choose turn out to be not so great after all, I can simply return them on my next visit.

One of the characters in Jean-Paul Sartre's *Nausea* is a huge bookworm and never returns a library book until he finishes it. The protagonist, Antoine, meets him at a library (of course). Antoine comes to realise that the man is reading every book in the library in alphabetical order, and he has been doing it for the past seven years.

That's shockingly ambitious. If someone were to tell me, 'I'll finish reading every book in this library in ten years,' I would stare at them with mouth agape. I'm not sure about you, but when I see someone extremely passionate, I become very conscious of the wide gap between us. And so, I much prefer the following quote from Alberto Manguel, who lives happily in his own library in France. In *The Library at Night*, he says the following:

> a library, whatever its size, need not be read in its entirety to be useful; every reader profits from a fair balance between knowledge and ignorance, recall and oblivion.[2]

I lack the fiery passion of the man in *Nausea*, so I'm content to check out a couple of books each time, depending on my mood that day. Whenever I feel like reading but don't exactly know what books I want, I go to the library. I take my time to explore the shelves, and if I find 'the one', it comes home with me.

Sometimes, I'm adventurous and borrow a book I don't usually read (I can always return it if I don't like it). Sometimes, I'm lucky to find a new release I've been dying to read (and if it's amazing, I buy a copy to keep). Sometimes, I search for a book that I had dropped midway previously (this time, it might be the right book!). Besides the fact that I cannot annotate library books, there isn't much difference between buying and borrowing. These days, I visit the library once or twice a week.

20

The Joy of Collecting Quotes

After finishing a book, I like to compile my favourite quotes. Sometimes I snap pictures, but if I'm in the mood, I type them out one by one in Evernote. The latter will take me an hour or two, but it's worth the immense sense of satisfaction. Sometimes I secretly wonder if I read because I want to collect more quotes. I'd hate to miss any good sentences.

Novelist Kim Young-ha once said that he wants to write a novel where the readers won't be underlining any sentences, but I think I'd be dismayed. He probably hopes that readers can lose themselves completely in the story and the emotions, but I love the thrill of chancing upon a line that truly resonates with me, or nudges me to reflect on my feelings, whether it's anxiety, confusion, or whatever. And I want to mark out those lines.

Every time I come across a sentence that describes exactly what I'm going through, I can't help but read it over and over. Do I have it in me to change things? Sometimes when I realise that it's impossible, that is in itself a life lesson. And when I see a particularly insightful quote, I sigh in relief. If I hadn't come across this nugget of wisdom, life might have turned out to be completely different.

Sometimes I imagine myself running in a field where the quotes are playing tag with me, waving at me to catch them. Depending on my mood and what I'm going through at that point, I search for different types of quotes. And when I catch one, I relish in the triumph, as though placing yet another piece in a jigsaw puzzle.

I have my favourite comfort quotes I fall back on. When I'm exhausted by the weight of the responsibilities on my shoulders, I find solace and escape in the following lines from Seneca's *On the Shortness of Life*:

> You will find no one willing to share out his money; but to how many does each of us divide up his life! People are frugal in guarding their personal property; but as soon as it comes to squandering time they are most wasteful of the one thing in which it is right to be stingy.[1]

Instead of settling down, I've become even more of a wandering soul. The following quote from Goethe's *Faust* acts like a guiding beacon of light in my life:

> Human beings wander for as long as we keep trying.[2]

There was a period of time when I found myself irked by humans, but the following quote from *Jeon Tae-il: A Biography* gives me hope that perhaps people aren't that bad after all:

No matter what it is, to not turn a blind eye is the essence of humanity.[3]

And when I question what it means to be an individual, I turn to Albert Einstein's notion that anything which is 'noble and sublime' arises not from the masses, or from herd mentality, but from the creativity and the dynamism of a single mind.[4]

After a disagreement with a friend, what pulled me out of wallowing in the past was this line from Mark Rowlands's *The Philosopher and the Wolf*:

When we think of memory, we overlook what is most important in favour of what is most obvious.[5]

Occasionally, when I fall into a deep sadness that I can't get out of, as though misery will stretch on for ever, I find strength in Shin Yeong-bok's *Contemplation in Prison*:

Even as we're gutted by sadness so painful that we want to crawl into a hole, bury ourselves in it and die, the amazing thing about life is that it takes only the smallest of joys to melt away the misery.[6]

And on days when I don't know what I'm doing with my life, I return to a quote from Annie Dillard's *The Writing Life*. As she says, our life is divided into days, and I can always start afresh every day:

How we spend our days is, of course, how we spend our lives.[7]

Confucius' *The Analects* is a quote collector's treasure trove.

To say you know when you know, and to say you do not when you do not, that is knowledge.

If wealth were a permissible pursuit, I would be willing even to act as a guard holding a whip outside the marketplace. If it is not, I shall follow my own preferences.

It is rare for a man to miss the mark through holding on to essentials.

As in the case of making a mound, if, before the very last basketful, I stop, then I shall have stopped. As in the case of levelling the ground, if, through tipping only one basketful, I am going forward, then I shall be making progress. [8]

The joy of reading extends beyond the last page of the book. If you see a quote that you like, write it down immediately, so that you can revisit it anytime. Sometimes a quote feels as though it's looking at us in the eye. Those who've experienced that will know what I mean. It's as if there's a beam of light shining upon us, guiding us just as we're feeling lost. Sometimes a single sentence is more powerful than a whole book.

21

Book Clubs

I like watching the Korean current affairs programme *Knowledge Channel ⓔ*. I remember an episode titled 'The Purpose of Examinations', which talked about the philosophy paper in the French Baccalauréat (the exam students in France sit for at the end of their secondary education). Students must choose between three short questions such as *Do we have the right to judge others? Is it possible to free ourselves from the past? Should we respect everyone?* and write a dissertation essay in four hours. The exam assesses the students' critical-thinking skills and ability to be members of society who can think and act for themselves.

It amazes me how much interest the average French person has in the exam. After the exam, when the year's questions are released, politicians share their answers on TV broadcasts, and scholars and citizens alike gather for passionate discussions. Everyone, whether it's on the streets, at the park or at home, is discussing philosophy.

Because the French are exposed to philosophical thought from a young age, they carry critical-thinking skills with them into adult life. That's very different from Korea, where we are taught rote memorisation. I can't quite imagine what it's like to be encouraged to think and voice our own opinions. But when I see how book clubs have sprung up in Korea recently, I wonder if things are starting to change.

A group of people who come together to discuss a book feels like a mini-Baccalauréat. Because of the way we Koreans were taught in school, we might not be as comfortable opening up immediately, but it feels like everyone is telling each other, 'It's OK. Don't be afraid of speaking your mind. There's no right or wrong. This is a safe space to think and grow together.'

There were book clubs I consistently attended, one for three years, another for a single year. Others, I only attended for a few sessions. I still remember my very first book club meeting. It was extremely awkward. Everything felt strange and unfamiliar; I had never sat down with a group of strangers to have a serious conversation. My heart thumped wildly at the thought that I needed to contribute something insightful to the discussion. I had rehearsed what I wanted to say, but when it was my turn to speak, everything tumbled out in an incoherent mess.

That was the first time it dawned on me that I was terrible at speaking.

I wanted to contribute, but I was nervous trying to find the right time to speak up. I wasn't the only one. We were all a little incoherent, but we were happy that we'd found a safe space to speak our minds – something that is difficult to do in our daily lives. The book club gave us a legitimate platform to express our true selves that we had to suppress.

The biggest charm of book clubs is how they encourage a difference in opinions. At the beginning, it felt uncomfortable to be openly disagreeing with each other, especially when the debate got a little heated. And it was upsetting when someone else shot down what I had thought was a well-thought-out argument. But soon, I came to realise how valuable this process is. Once I realised how I was holding on to certain convictions without any basis, I fell deeper into the joy of thinking critically.

One time, we read Hannah Arendt's *Eichmann in Jerusalem*. As one of the key individuals responsible for the Holocaust, which killed millions of Jews, Eichmann was a cruel mass murderer in the eyes of the public, but Arendt argues that it was more banal than that: he was thoughtlessly evil.

The longer one listened to him, the more obvious it becomes that his inability to speak was closely connected with an inability to think, namely, to think from the standpoint of somebody else. No communication was possible with him …[1]

Is it a crime not to be able to think critically? The participants discussed our responses to this question, sharing how close or far we felt we were from Eichmann, and how we could strive to live our lives differently from him. To ask and answer questions takes courage, and hopefully, we learn to think before we act.

22

Read to Seek Answers

When I first learnt that Aristotle believed that the ultimate purpose of human existence is happiness, I was shocked. I had never thought about chasing happiness. Was I the odd one out? The thought unsettled me so deeply that I desperately wanted to brush it off as nonsense – *What would he know anyway? He never spent a day of his life working!*

That said, I immediately went to read up on the theories of happiness. I had to know what exactly happiness was. But the more I read, the more unsure I became. In *Nicomachean Ethics*, Aristotle says the following:

Verbally there is very general agreement; for both the general run of men and people of superior refinement say this is happiness, and identify living well and doing well with being happy; but with regard to what happiness is they differ, and the many do not give the same account as the wise. For the former think it is some plain and obvious thing, like pleasure, wealth or honour; they differ, however, from one another – and often even the same man identifies it with different things, with health when he is ill, with wealth when he is poor ...[1]

Most people would probably think that the happy feelings we get on an ordinary day are 'happiness'. However, Aristotle differentiates between pleasure and happiness. According to his theories, happiness is achieved through virtuous activity and the development of one's potential. For example, someone who wants to be a pianist will only be happy when they finally achieve their goal. By contrast, philosopher Epicurus believes that pursuing pleasure leads to happiness. Here, we're talking about small pleasures in life. According to Epicurus, friendship, freedom and an examined life are crucial tools for achieving pleasure, and thereby happiness.

No two books share the exact same perspective when it comes to defining happiness. Some books talk about happiness as the 'experience of joy and meaning', and as for how to achieve happiness, one claims that it comes from a focused mind, while another believes that having wide-ranging interests, a robust coping mechanism, good health, positive relationships and regular exercise lead to happiness. I've even read somewhere that happiness is a life without suffering, and to become happier, instead of striving so hard, what we need is a prescription for anti-depressants. The Dalai Lama says that happiness comes from a peaceful mind and hence it's important to medi-tate. And according to Buddhist teachings, happiness is removing oneself from worldly attachments and desires.

Daniel Gilbert, Harvard College Professor of Psychology at Harvard University, writes about three types of happiness in his book *Stumbling on Happiness*. Gilbert distinguishes between emotional, moral and judgemental happiness. He defines emotional happiness as 'a *feeling*, an *experience*, a *subjective state*, and thus it has no object-ive referent in the physical world'.[2] Moral happiness refers to the satisfaction of living a virtuous life, while judge-mental happiness has nothing to do with one's changing moods on a daily basis but is the contentment that comes with looking back on life and feeling that one has done sufficiently well. The happiness we feel in life could be one of the trio or a mix of all three.

The different theories make me more confused, yet I also feel as though I'm getting closer to understanding what happiness is. That the most brilliant people in each field are trying various ways of understanding happiness underscores its importance, and seeing multiple ways of defining happiness makes me think that, at the end of the day, happiness is subjective. Another thing I've realised is that rarely does anyone know exactly how to achieve happiness. Perhaps, like freedom, everyone has the right to happiness, and we need to define it for ourselves.

It was only when I read Aristotle that I realised I've never sought out happiness. Was I ever happy? Maybe I did try looking for happiness. I decided to quit my job because I wasn't happy, and there were countless decisions I made based on my feelings. But because I had no idea what truly makes me happy, I couldn't become a happier person.

After reading so much on happiness, I started thinking about my own. I am happy when I'm taking an evening stroll in the sunset. Among the three types of happiness that Gilbert mentions, judgemental happiness is the most important to me. I have been contented with my life for the past few years, and I believe it means that I'm happy now. Some things that make me happy are good relationships, meaningful conversations, enough me-time, and doing a good job at work. Books taught me what my happiness looks like.

23

E-Books

These days, fewer people are reading books, but it doesn't mean that people have stopped reading altogether. In fact, people are reading more than ever on smartphones. Whether it's alone, with friends, on the subway, or even walking on the street – people are always on their phones, and if they're not watching a video or playing games, they're probably reading something.

I read often on my phone or on my laptop, but I am doubtful if it can be considered 'reading'. There has been much research claiming that when one reads on the internet there is a tendency to skip information, experience a shorter attention span, and absorb less compared to reading a physical book.

Jakob Nielsen, a web researcher, did a famous eye-tracking study of 232 participants reading web pages, and results show that we read very differently on devices versus books. Unlike reading books, where our gaze moves systematically from left to right and one line after the other, the participants' eye movements formed an 'F' shape. While they read to the end of the line at first, as they went down the page, they started skipping words, and at some point, they scanned the page in a vertical drop movement and claimed that they'd finished reading.

Try it. Are you reading carefully from left to right, sentence by sentence as you would when reading a book? Or are you simply doing a quick scan? Studies have shown that we read differently on the internet. Instead of parsing every sentence, we tend to zoom in on what we already know, and our eye movements form an 'F' shape as our gazes move downwards even before reading to the end of each line. Some people have the habit of leaving a standard comment on every article they read, something along the lines of, 'Nice one. Leaving a comment before I go.' Because of that, it feels like everyone's reading a lot. But in fact, they didn't even read the whole piece. And that is one of the limits of reading on a screen.

German academic Uwe Jochum, in *The History of All Books*, makes the bold claim that those who read on a screen – and that includes e-books – aren't readers but users. Canadian journalist David Sax echoes the sentiment in *The Revenge of Analog: Real Things and Why They Matter*. According to Sax, digital and analogue reading are two completely different experiences, and he asks readers to do him a favour. The book reads best when it is read in physical form – so when reading his book, please turn off your phone.[1]

Nevertheless, I still read on my devices every day, but I try to differentiate between texts that I'm OK to give a quick scan versus those I'd like to read carefully. On the internet, I may read in an 'F' or 'E' shape (reading the last few lines carefully), but if I feel like the article deserves my full attention, I make it a point to return to the first line for a second read – this time making sure I don't skip any word or sentence.

This year, I bought my first ever e-book. A journalist mentioned that they have different preferences when it comes to reading on the internet versus books – they are OK reading novels and essays on a device, but when it comes to philosophy or sociology texts, they get the physical copies. As for me, I think books similar to Malcom Gladwell's works – an easy read with interesting ideas and nuggets of insights – read well on the screen. Currently, I also have *Originals* and *Ego is the Enemy* on my e-bookshelf.

Why is it that physical books are easier to read than their electronic versions? To me, it's because of the 'constraints'. Unlike reading on devices, we don't get a touch function, neither can we switch to another app, add a bookmark, or use the word search. There's only us and the text. But with e-books, you have to impose restrictions on yourself. When I'm on my e-reader, I only allow myself to use the bookmark and highlighter functions. I want to dive deep between the lines and extract the meaning in every sentence, every word, and I don't want distractions.

24

Pockets of Free Time

My parents never pressured me in my studies, not even in high school when we were heading towards the most important exam of our lives – the Suneung, the university entrance exams. More than ten years have passed since then, but one day, out of curiosity, I turned towards my mum, who was peeling garlic in the living room. 'Mum, why didn't you force me to study?' She looked up and raised her eyebrows. 'As if you'd listen to me. If I had told you to study, you'd probably do the opposite.'

What she didn't say was: *Even now, you aren't gonna listen to me.* Instead of feeling apologetic (sorry, Mum!), I was grateful. If she'd forced me to sit down and study back then, I might have chosen to give up. But because she gave me the space, I studied in moderate amounts at the same time as I got to enjoy other hobbies. Even if I didn't excel at anything in particular (sorry again, Mum!), at least

I had fond memories of growing up with my favourite authors and books.

The first author I liked was German novelist Patrick Süskind. His books, which I read mostly in middle and high school, gave me an early taste of the loneliness that stemmed from simply living, and it helped me understand the emptiness that I struggled with at times. Whenever I got frustrated studying for the exams, I'd seek solace in a chapter or two from *Perfume* or *The Double Bass*. Suddenly, what I was going through seemed so insignificant, and at that thought, I felt better hitting the books again.

And if I still had trouble focusing, I'd think about Mr Sommer in *The Story of Mr Sommer*. We are never introduced to him properly, and all he does in the story is keep walking. He goes out before four in the morning, and only returns late at night, as if he's always being chased by an invisible being. Or maybe it's just himself. In the entire novel, he speaks only once, and only a single sentence, robustly proclaiming a wish to be left alone.[1]

I was nowhere near as wretched as Mr Sommer, but I lived vicariously through his outburst. Even though it wasn't directed at anyone, my moodiness dissipated, and I could go on to solve a few more problem sums.

I didn't start reading because I hated studying, although I'd admit that there was a period when I thought life would be so much better if I didn't have to study. Books accompanied me through every season in life, whether it was struggling with the convoluted English texts that would confuse even native speakers, feeling overwhelmed by the impending university entrance exams, desperately trying for a decent TOEIC score so as not to lose out at the starting line of the rat race, struggling to keep my eyes open on the way home after a long day at work. Whether it's waiting for the train, for the lift, at the hospital or the airport, I read. I am always busy, but I still find small pockets of time to read.

We'll never have 'enough time'. There are so many things competing for our attention, and we're always busy at work, juggling personal, familial and workplace relationships, and struggling to stay afloat amidst everything. Reading for hours feels like a luxury, an unrealistic dream. But don't forget, we still have time – it's just in fragments. Ten minutes before going to work, ten minutes after finishing lunch, thirty minutes on the way home, thirty minutes before bedtime. It may not be much, but it's still enough to read a few pages or a chapter.

In the time I wait for my hair to dry, I immerse myself in Leo Tolstoy's *Resurrection*. The story follows a man, Nekhlyudov, who sits on the jury to try a woman wrongly accused of murder. And when he realises that Maslova is the woman he had a past love affair with, and that his sins had turned her into the person she is right now, he falls into deep agony. I was swept up in the narrative as he went from realising his atrocities to wanting to atone for his sins by marrying her, all within four pages. By the time I looked up again, my hair had already dried, and I closed the book. Until the next time I picked it up again – and that might be a few hours or a few days later – the scene continued to echo in my mind. I no longer wait to 'have free time'. Instead, I have learnt to enjoy reading whenever I have a moment. And that's how I keep reading.

25

Read Slowly

A few years ago, I read a short travelogue where, instead of travelling to a different place, the author had 'travelled' through a painting by visiting the National Gallery in London. Initially, the plan was to stay at the gallery for just a few hours, but he got so engrossed in one of the paintings that he cancelled all other plans in order to visit the gallery every day for the rest of his trip.

The author was looking at the artwork, but perhaps in it he saw the turmoil within himself. What had given him pause, I wonder. But he might not have an answer, or he might struggle to make sense of it. Perhaps it would take a few more years, or until he gave in to the temptation to return to the gallery once more, that he would finally be able to say, 'The reason I stood in front of the painting was...'

I could imagine the same happening to a reader. As we read, we're confronting our inner selves. Just like looking at a painting, reading takes time. The time to gather the emotions that we didn't realise we've been suppressing, the forgotten feelings that return to shake our resolve. The time to digest our discomfort at being judged when we're trying to understand others, to embrace the excitement of feeling as though everything in the world is connected.

Because those who read need time to feel and understand the ripples reverberating in us, there's no point trying to rush and jump from book to book. Take your time; stay on a page and savour the words. There are how-to books out there introducing 'hacks' to increase reading speed, and when we've just made up our minds to get into the habit of reading, it's easy to fall into the impatience of wanting to read quickly and read more. But reading is about understanding the world and ourselves, not finishing as many books as possible. We aren't reading to become faster, but to feel and understand more. Unless you read for work, there's no reason to rush.

There are things that only those who slow down come to see – the gift that books give to those who gently savour each sentence. It's as if all the emotions and thoughts are stirring awake and talking to me. I take the time to respond, and suddenly, the part of me that was indifferent to the world fades away, leaving only the excitement thrumming in me. I close the book feeling as though I'm a step closer to understanding myself, and it's a feeling I've never got when I'm speed-reading.

Some books are not meant to be rushed through – books that bring out, in a few sentences, a shadow in me I hadn't realised existed; books that release the knots in my heart that I've been carrying for a long time; books that tug at me when I'm going too fast, nudging me to return to an earlier page.

For those of you who feel the need to take a walk several times a day, I recommend Frédéric Gros's *A Philosophy of Walking*. Why is it that you feel an urge to go somewhere? Why is it that you end up walking? Why do you feel alive again after a walk? If these are burning questions in your mind, pause your steps and read this. As for me, I took the time to think about why I love going on evening walks.

You are nobody to the hills or the thick boughs heavy with greenery. You are no longer a role, or a status, not even an individual, but a body, a body that feels sharp stones on the paths, the caress of long grass and the freshness of the wind. When you walk, the world has neither present nor future: nothing but the cycle of mornings and evenings. Always the same thing to do all day: walk.[1]

26

Life-Changing Reads

Whenever I see comments about a book being a 'life-changing read', my eyes light up. I read on to see if the person mentions which part(s) of the book had transformed their lives, and at the same time, a warm feeling spreads in my chest as I'm reminded of the numerous books that have become an indelible part of me.

In Korean, we have a phrase that translates directly to 'book of your life', which can mean a favourite read or a book that has a major influence on one's life. I don't really like to use this label, but there are books that have stayed with me, which can be loosely categorised into three groups. The first group are like the guardian angels in my life. Hermann Hesse's *Demian*, W. Somerset Maugham's *The Razor's Edge*, Henry David Thoreau's *Walden* and Erich Fromm's *The Fear of Freedom* are a few examples.

The second group consists of masterpieces that are exactly why I'll never stop reading. Books such as *Report to*

Greco by Nikos Kazantzakis, *The Elegance of the Hedgehog* by Muriel Barbery, *Stoner* by John Edward Williams. If someone asks me about my favourite books, I usually talk about these.

Last but not least are books that I enjoyed tremendously, stories that feel like the greatest reads in that moment, that I can't help but want to tell everyone around me about them. Books that step beyond the superficial descriptions of life, their prose brimming with sincerity. Some of the recent reads that fall into this category are: *The Beak of the Finch* by Jonathan Weiner, *The Quiet You*[1] by Choi Yoon-pil and *My Age of Anxiety* by Scott Stossel.

Every time I close a book and go, 'Wow, that was amazing!', I feel a heat spread in my heart, and I can practically hear the cogs in my brain whirring. *Which group should I put the book in? The second, or the first? All right, I'll go with the first.* I can't quite describe the feeling of finding yet another 'life-changing read'. It makes me feel a little surer in life, if you know what I mean?

Those who read appear more resilient than the average person because of the special books that we keep close to our hearts. Whenever I feel a little lost, I think about my favourite books. Instead of letting myself be swayed by others, I turn to books that have anchored me and continue to be a supportive presence in my life. And the more of such books I collect, the stronger I become.

Those who find books uninspiring may not have found the right ones that'll bring them joy, meaning or excitement. If you feel like this, why not change the types of books you've been reading? Be bold and go completely out of your comfort zone. Try a different genre or get a recommendation from your friends. And once you find that book that sparks something in you, you'll never feel the same about reading again.

I loved Lee Hwa-gyeong's *To Love, To Write, To Destroy*, a book about ten women writers who had it harder in life just because they were born as women and lived as women – Susan Sontag, Hannah Arendt, Rosa Luxemburg, Simone de Beauvoir, Ingeborg Bachmann, Virginia Woolf, George Sand, Françoise Sagan, Sylvia Plath and Jane Austen. Lee's foreword made an impression on me:

> What is important to the women is the clear understanding of themselves and their lives, knowing that they shouldn't live for others but for themselves … They bear the shackles of fate, but never once did they back down and give in. Amidst the stereotypes, the absurdity, and the exhaustion, they do not lose sight of the power of intellect and wisdom.[2]

Without a doubt, this book goes into the third group of life-changing reads.

27

Indie Bookshops

Several years ago, my friend sent me a couple of photos while she was travelling in Europe. One of them was taken at an indie bookshop that she had stopped by on an evening walk in Bologna, Italy. The photo captured a lovely moment – an elderly man with salt-and-pepper hair hosting a book club, his eyes bright with passion. I could almost see myself in my twilight years, taking an evening walk to the neighbourhood bookshop after dinner. I'd be content with a simple life like that.

Back then, indie bookshops in Korea were in decline. Just like the way we no longer see CD shops tucked away in the side streets, it seemed like we'd left behind the days where one could buy books anywhere. But in the last few years, we're seeing a surprising rebound, and instead of withering away, more and more indie bookshops, each with a unique identity, are popping up everywhere. There are even internet maps where people pin the locations of indie bookshops, the same way they would create a 'popular restaurants' map, and there are content creators and enthusiasts who go around the country visiting these bookshops. Occasionally, I chance upon one when out on a walk.

Every book lover has their personal favourites, and some even make a point of exploring local bookshops when travelling to other cities. The trend doesn't go unnoticed by big publishers. They design special editions that are only available at select indie bookshops, and it's increasingly common to see renowned authors giving book talks and holding book signings in small book-shops. Indie bookshops don't just sell books. They host a variety of activities, like book clubs, indie film screenings, and special events like 'Books & Beer' or 'Midnight Book Shopping'.

Why are indie bookshops back in fashion? Why do people start a bookshop business even though they know it's unlikely to be profitable? Are we no longer finding happiness in a life where 'more' and 'bigger' are the norm? Are we flocking to indie bookshops in the same way we seek out niche communities and hobbies? Is it because we want to free ourselves from capitalism and find something that better fits our life values? I don't have an answer, but in the same way that I'm inspired by my friend's photo, perhaps people are discovering something meaningful in indie bookshops.

A few days ago, I finally popped by an indie book-shop that I'd been meaning to visit. After getting off at Seolleung station on subway Line 2, I headed towards Choi Ina Books. The bookshop was located on the fourth floor of a building. To start a bookshop requires much courage – even more so in an obscure location like this. I was welcomed by a gentle piano melody. Everyone moved with quiet footsteps, browsing the shelves or reading in a corner. I went straight to the display racks.

The curation is what gives each indie bookshop its personality and reflects the owner's tastes and prefer-ences. Kim Young-geon, the third president of Donga Bookshop, which has now become a Sokcho city landmark in Gangwon-do, writes that curation is a challenging task because it's impossible to predict if your picks will reson-ate with readers:

> When you only push bestsellers and display the popu-lar books, great books get buried. So I ask myself – how can I introduce these gems to the customers?[1]

Excellent curation isn't about stocking what people are looking for, but books that they might not know about. There are many great reads out there waiting to be discov-ered; a good bookseller has a discerning eye for them. It's also not just about displaying the books on the shelves but taking the initiative to chat with customers before recommending something that they might enjoy. As Kim says in his book, a bookshop display, while seemingly small and insignificant, is a book desperately reaching out to us. The ball is in our court now. How do we respond?

Book recommendations by Choi Ina herself and her staff fill part of the wall display. Tucked between the pages is a handwritten note on why they love the book. It's a joy to read the notes, and for books that I'm interested in, I'll go on to read the introduction and a couple of pages, as usual. The book is talking to me, and I respond in kind. And, hopefully, my response will help – even if just a little – this lovely book sanctuary to stay with us for a long time.

28

The Next Book to Read

I attended the Seoul International Book Fair for the first time this year (2017). I was in awe at the huge crowd and the rows of booths that filled the spacious halls, not to mention the many ongoing book events. I had a great time checking out each booth and their curation for the fair. Two hours passed easily, and when it was almost five in the evening, I headed towards the 'book-clinic booth'.

I had signed up thinking that it would be a book talk, and it was only later that I realised it was literally a 1:1 session where you get a book prescription from a 'doctor'. I hesitated. Is it OK for a person writing about books to get a book prescription? But the next moment, my doubts ebbed. *So what? It might even be helpful!* I listened to the positive voice whispering to me, and soon, I was eagerly counting down to the date.

It turned out to be a very enjoyable thirty-three-minute conversation, at least from my perspective. Famed book critic Geum Jung-yeon was my 'doctor', and I was impressed by how much he knew about books and how he managed to keep the conversation flowing, even though I was jumping from one topic to another. He talked about several authors, and as I noted down the ones I was hearing for the first time, I couldn't help but wonder how many books he had read to date.

To Geum's question on whether I had a favourite author, I said a few names, out of which he wrote down only one on his notepad. Julian Barnes. Why did that particular name catch his attention? I watched his hand intently. Next to Barnes's name, Geum scribbled *'Flaubert's Parrot'*.

It was the title of one of Barnes's novels, touted to be a fictionalised biography of French writer Gustave Flaubert. Geum looked up at me with a smile.

'Do you know Gustave Flaubert?'

'Yes,' I said, nodding.

'Have you read *Madame Bovary*?'

I nodded again. Of course. *Madame Bovary* is Flaubert's representative work! Geum proceeded to draw four rectangles on the notepad and connected them with lines. He hadn't written anything inside the rectangles, but I immediately knew what he meant. Julian Barnes, *Flaubert's Parrot*, Gustave Flaubert and *Madame Bovary*. He was trying to show me the connection between the books and authors.

Books stand alone as unique works, yet they are also interconnected. If one understands *Flaubert's Parrot's* deep links with Gustave Flaubert, reading that and *Madame Bovary* one after another can be very intellectually stimulating. In his essay collection *Exceptional Writing Always Wins*, Geum says the following:

> I've published three books so far, but it'd be a lie to say that I wrote them alone. No one can write a book entirely by themselves. Just like the authors whose books I quote from.[1]

Many of us write because we're inspired and influenced by the books that we've read. In that sense, we are never writing alone. I imagine a line of writers holding hands across time and space. If we can understand how the books are connected, we can read with greater depth.

Instead of moving on to the next book immediately, spend some time thinking about what you liked about it; maybe there are connections with other books waiting to be discovered. If you enjoy a particular author's ideas and thoughts, go and find out if there are authors whom they admire. Or, with other books on topics that you enjoy, if a certain quote lingers in your mind, check out the source texts. Books are like a spider's web: you'll only get more attached.

29

Read When You're Happy, When You're Anxious, and in the Moments in Between

After graduating with a degree in computer science, I found a job as a software engineer for the mobile-phone brand of a major conglomerate. At first, I had no idea what I was supposed to do, but after going through the new-hires training and starting the job proper, I realised it was quite straightforward. Sit at my assigned desk, turn on the company laptop, and code from morning till evening.

Save for the occasional business trip, I was desk-bound most of the time. My job was to fine-tune the phone software's functionality. Never once had I pause to think, *What should I do at work today?* Work was automatically assigned to me, and on payday, my salary was credited directly to my account.

But right now, life couldn't be more different. I'm doing something completely unrelated to my major, and I have no boss to answer to. No one is here to instruct me to write, nor am I subjected to anyone's expectations or appraisal. I spend every day with language and words. I sit down at the desk that my parents bought me during university and use my own laptop. Instead of programming languages, I'm working with spoken languages – Korean.

Unless I'm on a holiday, I stay in my room almost all the time, reading or writing. Every day, I wake up thinking: *What should I write today?* On days when I barely produce anything, I go to bed feeling depressed and guilty. If I don't make work for myself, there's nothing to do, but even when I'm working, I'm not earning consistently every month. Despite that, I'm happier with my life now. Because it's what I wanted.

I'm still desk-bound, using a laptop and working with languages, but apart from that, everything is completely different. The work environment, my daily routine, my social status, how much I have in my bank account, how often I meet and talk to others ... Sometimes it feels like I've become a completely different person in the past few years.

Whenever I mention that I quit my job, I always get the same question.

'How did you find the courage to leave?'

And my answer is always: 'Well, I simply quit.'

To me, it was the most natural thing to do at that point. Not that I hadn't fretted over the decision, but because

I had no idea what exactly I was worried about, I didn't know what else to answer.

But when I read Erich Fromm's *To Have or To Be?*, it dawned on me that perhaps I was trying to choose between 'what I have' and 'who I am'. Fromm makes a distinction between the two:

> If I am what I have and if what I have is lost, who then am I? Nobody but a defeated, deflated, pathetic testimony to a wrong way of living ... If I am who I am and not what I have, nobody can deprive me of or threaten my security and my sense of identity.[1]

Instead of being on the extreme ends of the spectrum, I probably oscillate in between. In the daytime, I'm happy to be true to myself, but at night, I start to worry that I have less than my peers. And probably I'll keep feeling this way for years to come, but that's only my guess. And because I swing in between happiness and anxiety most of the time, this means a particularly good day will feel extra blissful, doesn't it?

30

Movies and Novels

I was incredibly lucky to have had the chance to interview Korean novelist You-jeong Jeong. It was around the time her novel *The Good Son*[1] was published and I thought I would take the opportunity to read all her works. Her novels are wildly popular, and understandably so. Reading them is akin to watching a film, and I was immediately drawn into the worlds that she had created.

During the interview, she shared that *Seven Years of Darkness*[2] was getting a big-screen adaptation. *Of course the producers would be interested*, I thought. When I was reading the book, I found myself thinking about the actors that'd fit the roles, and if an average reader like me could see a film being born out of the novel, it would immediately jump out at the professionals! As we chatted about film adaptations, I told her who I thought might be suitable to play the titular character Yu-jin in *The Good Son* – a young actor whose features embody both kindness and evil, weakness and cruelty, with strong acting skills, who can morph into any of his roles. That was how much of an impression the character had made on me.

I love watching film adaptations, especially of books that I've enjoyed. I want to see how well the movie manages to visualise the characters and bring the story to life. A good narrative flow is important, but my focus is always on the characters – how similar or different they are from how I'd imagined them, and if the actors manage to capture the nuances. It's also interesting to see which character traits the director chooses to bring out, and what they tone down or change.

If I watched the movie first and see a particularly charismatic or unique character, I might read the novel to see how the author had described their appearance or personality. Colm Tóibín's *Brooklyn* and Austin Wright's *Tony and Susan* are two books I've read this year after watching their big-screen adaptations.

I can't be the only one falling for Tony (played by Emory Cohen) in *Brooklyn*, right? He's such a hopeless romantic, yet he's not just besotted. He's capable and charismatic, speaking and acting with perfect poise – never too much, nor too little. He has that smooth, natural charm about him. When I read the novel, I was delighted to see Tony described exactly this way. Cohen did a tremendous job with his character! In the novel, the female main character Eilis describes Tony as looking 'delighted', and if you've watched the movie, you'll know exactly what she means.

Nocturnal Animals, adapted from *Tony and Susan*, follows the story of Edward, an unpublished author, seeking revenge on his ex-wife, Susan, who abandoned him years ago. Years after their separation, he sends her a manuscript titled *Nocturnal Animals* (his nickname for her) and asks her to read it. She does and is quickly consumed by the life of main male character, Tony Hastings. When I was watching the film, I was curious about what Tony was like in the novel. But when I finally read it, I found myself thinking about the relationship between Susan and Edward, and how a novel connects them again after years of non-contact. And how Edward gets his revenge by winning over the heart of the reader. Susan is plunged into emotional turmoil after reading the novel, and it's a meta reference to us readers, who are likewise taken in by the story within the story.

> Reading pushes through the sea like a swimmer. The creatures of Susan's daylight mind, animals of land and air, sink into it, converted into dolphins, submarines, fish. Something bites her while she swims, a small toothy shark. She needs to drag it into the air where she can see.[3]

31

Let's Discuss Books

One of my favourite Korean variety shows is the popular *The Dictionary of Useless Knowledge*, because who doesn't love a good battle of wits among five men? My friend watches it too, and she quipped that the programme made her realise how ignorant she was of the world. I chuckled. She's not the only one.

I'm impressed by their knowledge, analytical skills and quick wit, but when I was watching the programme, I found myself thinking, *Wow, this is the perfect environment to have book discussions.* I imagined a get-together of book lovers sharing their favourite quotes while enjoying a drink. I wished I had something like that!

If you're surrounded by book lovers, chances are you'll also be reading. Just as buddy reads double the fun of reading, it's extra fun to be able to have an intellectually stimulating book discussion with friends. But sadly, most of the time, your excitement for books isn't going to be reciprocated. That's why people end up feeling that reading is a solitary activity, something that they don't mention when they're with friends. Not just friends. In their essays, several bibliophiles have mentioned being punished by their parents for reading 'too much'.

Do I see you nodding along? If so, what you can do is take small steps to change the environment for yourself. Perhaps get a good friend to buddy read with you. Make a special trip to the bookshop. Choose a book that both of you are interested in. Find a café and add some fun by betting a coffee on how long you can read for. Feel free to chat anytime; there are no rules saying you can only discuss a book after finishing it.

The other day, I was buddy reading with my friend.

'Did you see that bit on page 56? It's exactly me right now. Is it the same for you?' my friend asked.

'Oh? I've finished that page, but I don't recall what the author said. Which bit is that?' I replied.

Most people tend to talk about how a book makes us feel in general, but our conversation made me realise the importance of distilling ideas and thoughts nestled within individual pages, and how a particular sentence can also add meaning to our lives. And to do that with a friend makes for a meaningful experience. Thanks to her, I got to revisit a point that I had missed on page 56, and I loved our subsequent discussion.

Besides encouraging my friends to read with me, I like choosing books for them as gifts. If I think that a book would be helpful to the situation they are facing, I try my best to persuade them to read it. I even got two of my friends to read Leo Tolstoy's *Anna Karenina* with me. It's thanks to years of effort that I can now easily talk about books with people around me.

Perhaps because my friends are also craving a good read, they agree readily whenever I ask them to buddy read with me. But because everyone's busy with kids, work and whatnot, we allow ourselves three months for each book. And as we discuss the books, we also end up sharing our personal lives and become even closer to one another. Books help us open up and dive into deeper topics.

In his essay collection *A Fool in Love with Books*, famed bibliophile and Silhak scholar Lee Deok-mu, from the late Joseon dynasty, says that reading with friends brings more joy than reading alone.

At the right time, with the right friends, with the right book and having a conversation that feels just right in the moment. This is unparalleled joy, but why is such happiness so rare?[1]

I agree.

32

Reading Multiple Books at Once

'I read only one book at a time. Reading multiple books at the same time feels as though I'm not respecting any of them,' said a friend.

There are many people who are loyal partners in reading. They hold on to the belief that one has to see the relationship through to the end before moving on to a new book. They insist that this is the right thing to do, to give our full attention to each book.

I hesitantly confessed that I have an 'open relationship' with books, and I was reading more than five books. My friend stared at me with rounded eyes. 'Wait, you read five?! Is that possible?' And I replied right away, 'Of course.'

I used to think that reading one book at a time was the way to go, but I've discovered a different way to love, and there's no turning back. The question now isn't one versus multiple, but *how many* I can read at once. Too many and it can get taxing, but too few and I'll be bored.

Six or seven is the maximum, and usually I can comfortably read three to five at any one time. You may wonder if I get distracted easily, but there's only one downside to this method: reading some books faster than others. I sometimes forget that I'm reading a book and it's not until months later that I notice a slight bulge in one of the books and a pencil rolls out from between its pages. How did it end up on the bookshelf?

Just the other day, I found a pencil at page 48 of *Yoga for People Who Can't Be Bothered to Do It* by Geoff Dyer. The following line on the Korean-edition cover caught my attention: *Heal by walking through the ruins.* I didn't want travel essays that are beautiful and aspirational; I wanted something raw, honest. This book had my heart right from the first page. The author is a middle-aged man struggling with an existential crisis, and he travels through ruins as practice for the rough times ahead.

Are you struggling with your current read but feel obliged to keep reading? Are you stealing glances at the other books you wish you were reading instead? If so, just stop and reach for the other book. There isn't a right or wrong way to read.

33

Reading Silently vs Reading Aloud

A person is reading quietly in the corner. Nothing else matters in that moment: the world is just them and their book. William Somerset Maugham's *The Razor's Edge* perfectly captures this vibe. In the story, the first-person narrator sees Larry reading in his club's reading room. He's been there since the morning, and when the narrator leaves the room late in the afternoon, he's still reading. Curious, the narrator goes back in the evening, only to see that Larry is still there. The narrator can't help but marvel at his incredible ability to focus.

What if Larry were a real person, and the narrator were the theologian and philosopher Augustine of Hippo (354–430 CE)? What would be shocking to him wouldn't be how long Larry spent focusing on the book, but the fact that Larry was reading silently. I imagine Augustine of Hippo hovering around Larry, observing him with interest.

In *The Confessions*, Augustine of Hippo describes seeing people reading silently. In the past, whether it was someone reading alone in a room, with a group of friends, sitting on a rock in a stream or in the library, people used to read aloud. Perhaps there were some who read silently, but according to *A History of Reading* by Alberto Manguel, *The Confessions* was the first record of silent reading.

It was only from the tenth century that silent reading gained popularity. People started to discover its advantages, such as the way it helped them to think and focus.

As time passed, silent reading became the norm. Unless it's a teacher calling upon a student to read aloud in class or at an author's reading, people rarely vocalise when reading. But does that mean that silent reading is the superior method? Not necessarily. Jae C. Choe, a professor of EcoScience, says he likes to imagine himself as a voice actor and read aloud his work. And because doing so slows him down, he finds it easier to remember what he has read.

I read silently most of the time, but despite *A History of Reading*'s claim that reading aloud is distracting, I read aloud to gather my thoughts. Not aloud in the sense that others can hear me, but I move my lips, vocalising each sound and syllable as I follow the text. Sometimes I move my lips in silence. I do that for a couple of pages, as if to reclaim all the scattered attention, and once my mind is sharp again, I switch back to silent reading.

These days, I'm seeing book clubs holding read-aloud sessions. It's great to see that people are recognising the advantages of reading aloud and accepting that there are different ways to read. Who says that we can only read in one way?

34

Read Books That Resonate

When I started to read *The First Thing You See*, I was reminded of the romantic comedy *Notting Hill*. At first, it looked like a romance about a young car mechanic, Arthur (who's described as being as handsome as Ryan Gosling), transcending all barriers to be together with Hollywood starlet Jeanine, who bears an uncanny resemblance to Scarlett Johansson. But I knew Grégoire Delacourt was not about to write a sweet love story. I knew a twist was coming, and I was right. At the novel's core is the theme of exploring identity in love.

Appearance matters a lot in society. But what do two very good-looking people see when they look at each other? And what happens when they fall in love? Despite their flawless features and striking looks, they are carrying a lot of pain inside. What do they hope their partner can see in them? This is a story about pain, and it is a powerful reminder that love is about understanding and empathy, and the ability to see beyond physical appearance for a deeper connection. In the novel, when Jeanine confesses her past, Arthur hugs her tight.

> He felt deeply sad … the only thing he could do, the only vocabulary he could draw on, was to hold her close. It was pure and chaste.[1]

In *We Only Saw Happiness*, also a Grégoire Delacourt novel, the narrator shoots his daughter on the happiest day of their lives. He turns to shoot his son when, suddenly, the daughter, who he thought was dead, opens her eyes. He looks at his blood-drenched daughter and shouts at his son to call the ambulance.

He wants his children to leave the world carrying happy memories. He loves them too much: that's why he tries to kill them.

Will readers understand such a horrific act? I cannot condone his actions, but I empathise with him. I feel his sadness, his loneliness, his pain, so much that I want to reach out through the pages and hold his hand tight.

We read because we want to be understood. And don't we all wish that the person we love will be able to see the pain we are carrying? And when the characters in the novel hug each other, somehow it feels like we're being comforted too.

We read to understand others. To understand someone else is empathy. That person might not have anything in common with us at all. He may be a monstrous being who shoots his own daughter, but like us he also carries deep pain within him. In that sense, we can transcend our individual selves and experiences to empathise with his circumstances.

Empathy, whether given or received, is important. To understand that some things are universal, but at the same time to accept individual differences. When we're able to empathise with others, we're also learning to embrace ourselves positively, and to spread that positivity to others. When we try to understand others, they do the same for us, and that's how we bond. Good books teach us empathy and connect each of us.

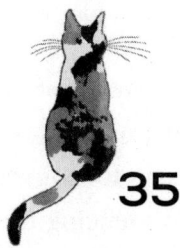

35

Read Beyond Success and Failure

To observe myself objectively, sometimes I imagine myself as a fictional character. When I do that, it's as if I'm looking at 'me' through a camera. In a novel, what type of character would I be? My life is too plain for me to be the main character, but at the very least I can play a small role, right? I don't think I'm the type that causes trouble for the protagonists. Maybe I'm the bluntly honest friend that rubs others up the wrong way?

Just like I analyse characters in a novel, I am better able to observe myself from a distance. I may not be Nina in Luise Rinser's *Mitte des Lebens*, but I can probably be an ex-classmate who admires her. Why so? Well, if Nina is someone who gives everything to live a vivid, colourful life, I'm the type who realises, belatedly, how plain my life is and then feels a lingering regret that I hadn't done more.

I wonder what authors are thinking when they write a novel. Do they want to put a bit of themselves inside?

And those who name a character after themselves – is that their way of finding purpose in storytelling? In *What Authors Do*, Kim Yeon-su says for some authors, the stories they read go beyond influencing their lives. He, too, has experienced transformational changes.

According to Kim, stories are born out of characters seeking what they don't have, which is why you'll never get a perfect character who already has everything. We read about their struggles, their efforts, and the higher they aspire, the more intense the stories get. From there, Kim realises something:

> Ultimately, it's either a happy ending or a sad one ... Life, too, doesn't care whether you succeed or fail in the end. What's important is how you choose to live each day, what you learnt, and the kind of stories you want to fill your life – these are the important questions.[1]

I turned his words over and over in my mind. Indeed, we only live life once. It's what we do each day that determines the life we lead. Many people have tried chasing the North Star, but no one has ever reached it. Does it matter? Just by trying, their lives shine.

When I imagine myself as a novel character, I crave the infinite possibilities of life. To step away from the dichotomy of success and failure, and stop judging a person's life based on their achievements or mistakes. I read to live in the moment, with no care about winning or losing. I read to practise seeing myself and others from a third, fourth, and even a fifth perspective.

My life, even as a fictional character, may not be the most colourful, but in my own ways I'm making consistent efforts. Won't that earn me at least an average mark? I may not have much, but I won't let that bother me. Someone reading the novel might wonder what gave me the confidence to be so relaxed and carefree. And they will come to realise at the end of the novel that there's actually no particular reason – and that in itself is a small plot twist.

36

Read During the Holidays

July is coming to an end. The other evening, I was out with my friends. I had a delicious bowl of cold naeng-myeon noodles, and after dinner we walked to a pub nearby. I ordered a pale ale, and the hint of bitterness made it extra delicious. Through the huge windows, I could almost feel the heat outside. Just as I was thinking how sitting in the cool blast of the air-conditioning with a bunch of good friends felt like a summer holiday, someone asked, 'What's everyone doing for the summer break?' There was a murmur of replies, but no one had concrete plans.

The conversation then turned to what we'd done last summer. Before long, it was getting late. Only then did I start to think about the earlier question. What should I do this summer? *Oh well, it would be nice to just lie in bed all day and read.*

'Aren't you already reading every day?' I can hear your thoughts from the other side of the book. You may be wondering if I'm only saying this because I'm not travelling (I have to work on the book the entire summer), but I'm really telling the truth. There's nothing I want to do more than to relax the entire day with a book that's set somewhere near a sea or lake. (Yes, it must have a large body of water.) In his book *The Anatomy of Bibliomania*, Holbrook Jackson says of the author George Gissing:

> Nothing gave him greater pleasure than the thought that there were times when he could *sit reading, quietly reading all day long*; 'tis a common dream of them all whether it comes true or not, they would be reading *a mane ad noctem usque*[*].[1]

I used to keep my holidays busy. I'd start planning months in advance, hoping to make every minute count, and impatiently count down to D-day. Not now. These days, I want to slow down, to stop rushing here and there, to stop cluttering my mind, and to stop trying so hard all the time. And if I make plans, I make sure it's something I truly like. And that is to laze in bed and read.

In the evening, when the summer heat lingers, I turn on the fan, position it near my head, lie flat on my stomach, and read *Adventures of Huckleberry Finn*. It's the story I need to beat the relentless summer heat. I imagine

* Latin: 'from morning until night'

myself drifting down the Mississippi River on a raft. With a plate of cut fruits and a can of beer within reach, I follow Huck and Jim's adventures as they confront the world with wisdom and courage.

Things aren't that much better now, but last year I went through a particularly rough patch, and I was worrying all the time. But I told myself that at least over the holidays, I should let go of everything. It's the time to put aside our daily worries and to-do list, and simply rest. And I want to do just that – to let my body and mind have its deserved break.

This year, for two days, I will shut down my laptop, tuck in my chair and spread a soft blanket on the floor. I will position a small fan on the right of my pillow, and a palm-sized one on the left, and wear my most comfortable clothes. Then I'll lie down with a book of my choice. A book that smells of the cool, refreshing ocean.

In *The Anatomy of Bibliomania*, Jackson says: 'The time to read is any time.' I agree, but I will say this: 'The time to read is any time, but the best time to read is during a holiday.'

37

The Flavours of Words

My friend, a Korean language and literature teacher, says she can't stand bad writing. If she spots several mistakes, or if the sentences are clumsy, she will give up reading immediately. She doesn't trust translated texts and insists on reading only Korean authors. At first, I thought that was rather extreme, but now that I've developed a sharper sense of language, I've become as particular as her.

Limp, awkward sentences make me tired. Even if the content is great, once the delivery falls short I have no choice but to give up midway, and that's especially true when it comes to translated texts. When we don't understand what we're reading, we tend to blame ourselves first, but in fact, it could be that the translation is awkward. While I may not be able to pinpoint what's lacking, the sentences simply don't vibe with me, and I find myself pausing at odd turns of phrase every now and then.

For a while, I blamed my sharpened sensitivity towards language for not being able to enjoy reading like I used to. But on the other hand, I've also come to better appreciate good writing. Great prose makes me squeal with delight.

Now that I am used to looking beyond the generic structure of a text to focus on the individual sentences, I'm having a lot more fun reading. I love discovering Korean authors whose writing is polished. In Korean, we describe such prose as seryeonha-da – elegant.

How then, do we develop an eye for good writing? The answer is simple: read good writing. When I think of people who are particular about the craft of writing, novelists come to mind. Every author has a different style, and as you keep reading, you'll naturally recognise good sentences and develop your own preferences.

Lee Kiho's writing stands out among Korean authors. I haven't finished all his books, but so far I've enjoyed everything he has written. Just look at the first few lines of *A Consultation* from his short-story collection *I Try to Be Indifferent*. Simple, yet not bland.

When the winds start to have a touch of chill, some people may think, Ah, it's autumn. Not me. I go – Damn, it's this time of the year again. Because I'm an elementary-school teacher.[1]

Kim Hyeri, a *Cine21* journalist, is also one of my favourite writers. Her prose is elegant, and she knows how to vary the length of her sentences. This makes her writing dynamic and a joy to read. I love the following paragraph in the film magazine where she writes about the beautiful and heart-fluttering reunion scene in the movie *Moonlight*, when Chiron arrives at Kevin's after a long drive:

Time seems to become viscous; the heartbeat slows, and the truth unravels. They've come a long way to adulthood, I thought to myself. For the viewers who've followed Chiron through his thirty years of life, we can finally release the breath we've been holding.[2]

38

Parents Who Read

People often say that if the parents are well-read, their children are likely to become readers. I don't think that's always true. After all, it's not uncommon to read about writers or bibliophiles lamenting that their children didn't inherit the same love for books.

But in my case, my parents are the reason I've grown to love reading. When my sister was still a toddler, a neighbour once asked her, 'What does your mum do at home?' and she answered, 'Mummy is always reading or sleeping.' That's right. Even now, Mum likes to read on the bed or sofa. I found myself nodding at what Anne Fadiman, who comes from a family of bookworms, says in *Ex Libris*:

My daughter is seven, and some of the other second-grade parents complain that their children don't read for pleasure. When I visit their homes, the children's rooms are crammed with expensive books, but the parents' rooms are empty. Those children do not see their parents reading, as I did every day of my childhood.[1]

Quiet hours at our house start at 10 p.m. When I was a kid, there was nothing much to do except read. My dad wasn't particularly strict when it came to our studies, but we couldn't watch TV anytime we wanted. After nine, the TV was off limits to us. My parents would turn off the TV after watching the news, and by ten, our house was completely quiet. Sometimes the silence was so deafening that I wanted to be anywhere else but in my own room.

In a house so quiet that I felt obliged to walk on tiptoes, there was really nothing to do except to sleep or read. I'm not a radio person, unlike my sister, so that was not an option for me. I usually stayed in my own room, my older sister in hers, and my parents in the master bedroom. Sometimes my mum did her own thing in the living room, but basically, it was me-time for everyone until bedtime.

My parents have never forced me to read. Nor did they read me bedtime stories like in the movies. My parents read, but they've always been readers – not only in order to be role models to us. I watched them as a kid (like I said, there wasn't much to do at home) and naturally picked up the habit. So, in that sense, I read because my parents do.

In *Ex Libris*, Fadiman also shares a touching and warm story about her family. Her father, eighty-eight years old, is also an author, and one day, he goes blind after suffering from retinal necrosis. Fadiman takes care of him, and late one night her father, who is still working as an editor and critic, says:

'I don't wish to be melodramatic, but you should know that if I can't read or write, I'm finished.'

And Fadiman replies.

'Well, Milton wrote *Paradise Lost* after he went blind.'

Her father thinks back to Milton's famous sonnet 'On His Blindness', and after she returns home, Anne reads him the beautiful sonnet over the phone. He listens quietly.

My parents have also been very supportive. Back when I wanted to leave my job at thirty years old, I confessed to them that I was too exhausted, and I was at the end of my rope. Instead of stopping me, they told me this: 'I read a book recently. It says times have changed and, in your generation, it's common to switch jobs several times. You're only on your first one. It's OK to quit. This time, find something you want to do.'

39

Read Widely, Then Deeply

Once I showed my half-yearly book-tracker list to a cultural critic well-versed in East Asian classics. His advice was: 'You read widely. That's great. But you should go more in depth.'

I glanced through my list. There was a range of novels and non-fiction titles. Only a couple of business and economics reads, but overall, a balanced mix of humanities, social sciences and natural sciences titles. I could see why the critic thought my reading repertoire 'lacks depth'.

That was during a time when I was making a conscious effort to read widely. I used to read only novels and essay collections, and I was trying to branch out into different genres like social sciences, philosophy and psychology. I tucked away the critic's advice for the time being.

A philosopher once said that in order to dig deep, one has to dig wide first. I like how it validates what I was doing. And don't first-year students usually take general courses before selecting their specialisations in the second year? Breadth comes before depth.

That's why I chose to read widely first, and I would recommend doing the same. If you've been reading novels, pick a non-fiction book instead. If you've read several natural science titles in a row, branch out into something different – maybe a psychology essay collection? When you have enough breadth, then it's time to go deep.

One of the books in the list I showed the critic was *The Selfish Gene*, and recently, I've been rereading it. According to the author Richard Dawkins, the animal is a survival machine for its genes. We exist to pass on our genes to the next generation. Devout religious thinkers have criticised Dawkins, but personally, I like how the book makes me conscious of the genes I carry, and it gives me a little comfort about my existence in this wide world.

I was struck by Dawkins's theory about 'memes' – a term he coined. Humans evolve across generations, but according to Dawkins, evolution can also take place within a generation as memes are transmitted quickly from one mind to another.

Examples of memes are tunes, ideas, catch-phrases, clothes fashions, ways of making pots or of building arches. ... If the idea catches on, it can be said to propogate itself, spreading from brain to brain.[1]

Memes also compete with one another for the human brain's attention.

Next time someone asks me why I believe in reading widely first, I'm going to reference Dawkins. Before a single meme dominates my attention, I need to gather wisdom from a wide variety of sources, and only when I am able to strike a balance between them will I turn my focus to a single meme. And that's how to train cognitive flexibility.

40

Keep a Reading List

I have a monthly book list where I write down the titles I've read and number them accordingly. At first, I just wanted to track the number of books I'd read, but I soon realised that a reading list is more useful than that. Not only does it allow me to understand my reading patterns and speed, filling in the list also motivates me to read more.

A few months ago, I found out that a friend of mine keeps a list of the movies – mainly arthouse and indie films – that he's watched. We were talking about our favourite movies when he whipped out his smartphone and scrolled through his list, telling me I should watch *The Lobster*, a dark comedy about a bachelor who moves into a hotel with other single individuals, where they have to find a romantic partner within a time limit or be turned into animals.

When we met again recently, I asked if he also kept a reading list, and he made an expression as though

I'd asked the obvious. He showed me his list. 'Why do you only read novels?' I asked. He cocked his head and thought hard. 'I guess I enjoy fiction? But sometimes I read only because I want to fill the list.' My eyes rounded slightly. I thought I knew what he was about to say. 'If the list is empty, my heart feels empty, too.'

Mid-month is when I'm the most anxious. It's the time I look back at what I've read in the past two weeks and decide on my goals for the latter half of the month. Unless there is an emergency, I get upset when I see that I've only read three or four books. Because that means I will need to catch up by reading more than six in the next fortnight in order to hit my goal of reading at least a dozen books a month. Even though no one else is going to see my list, I'll fluff it up by putting in the titles I'm only starting to read, or even what I hope to read. And for the next two weeks, I deliberately choose to read thin books. I know it's silly, but I can't help it. I absolutely cannot stand an empty list.

Popular Korean portal sites have their own sections devoted to book recommendations from famous person-alities, such as 'The Scholar's Bookshelf' and 'Celebrity Reads'. Usually the recommendations include life-changing reads, but personally, I'm more interested in books that people, whether a scholar, celebrity, or average person like you and I, have read but later forgotten.

These ordinary books might not have transformed our lives, but they've still given us something, filling the gaps in our lives and perhaps guiding us to take a road we'd otherwise not have chosen. When I'm stuck in the doldrums, these books tell me their stories, like a strict but kind teacher giving me advice. I make a list so that I won't forget these books.

Jean Grenier, in *La vie quotidienne*,[1] says that books are like a guide in life. Books are friends we make along life's journey. And as the French political philopsopher Charles de Montesquieu says, 'I have never known any distress that an hour's reading did not relieve.' I want to remember the book that has healed me today.

41

Read to Live the Life You Want

'You can't understand how I feel.'

Despite saying that, my friend went on to tell me about her six years of marriage, their cramped rented apartment, her struggle with infertility, how she felt like a failure compared to her friends, and her fear that she'd never be able to attain her dream life.

I've not been married, so my friend was right to say that I couldn't fully understand her worries. But I tried my best to comfort her. 'Look at me. I haven't achieved half as much as you, and I'm still living well.' It didn't help at all, not when she was only focusing on what she didn't have and aiming for something she couldn't reach.

It wasn't that her friends' lives were perfect. Their apartments might be bigger, but as the saying goes, 'only the living room is mine; the rest belongs to the bank'. Someone's daughter might be having trouble adjusting to school. Maybe the husband and wife have been giving each other the cold shoulder for more than a week. Everyone has their own issues, it's just that they aren't talking about them.

Everyone else is moving forward while I'm still at the starting line – I feel this way all the time, too. It doesn't matter if I'm earning well or not, or whether I love or hate my job. The mood envelopes me all the same. But when one chooses to fixate on a problem, the problem seems to grow larger than life, and life itself turns into a problem. And because I'm struggling in my own pit, I can't see the shadows shrouding the lives of others, or maybe I just don't want to care.

We see what others choose to show us. We see the curls in their hair, but not the tangles in their hearts. I'm in pain, but others are hurting too. I pretend to be fine; others are also hiding their pain. That's how we fall for the illusion that others aren't suffering as much as we are. We only see our own pain; we magnify our own sense of injustice.

That's why we need writers. They tell our stories, putting in words what we dare not say for fear of revealing our weaknesses and being judged. They are here to remind us that in life, light and darkness exist side by side. In the epilogue of *The Right to Study*, Jung Yeoul says:

My bio paints a picture of a smooth-sailing life. ... But that's because you can't expect me to write this: The fear of being ostracised, depression and negativity make up 80% of me. My bio is the perfect disguise to hide my true self.[1]

Desperation, despair, anxiety, emptiness, pessimism. Masked or otherwise, the emotions are still within us. To read is to embrace both the light and the darkness in my life, and the lives of others.

Whether it's the moments of fulfilment or sadness, the complex but humane characters, or the happiness and suffering that permeate the stories, books are a reflection of our lives. And it's such wisdom we need.

If we can understand life, we're freeing ourselves from obsessing over what we lack. Instead of focusing on the glamorous lifestyles of others and feeling as though we're never enough, we learn to realise what we truly want.

42

Read Book Reviews

I love reading what people write about books, be it a review, personal essay or critique piece. When I read about what others are thinking, feeling and taking away from the texts, I'm thinking, feeling and learning with them. Sometimes I'm impressed by their tastes and perspectives, and at other times I find myself rebutting their arguments in my mind. It's as if I'm having a conversation with them through the prose.

I read, on average, two book reviews a day, but when I'm completely absorbed in it, I can spend an hour reading one after another. Sometimes it's several reviews of the same book, or if I like the author's style, multiple pieces they've written. (I'm not referring only to reviews written by book critics, but anyone in general.)

Critic Lee Hyunwoo says that reviews help to sieve out the books that are worth reading, and I agree. After reading a review, I have two options: to read the book, or not.

Because I'm easily swayed, I came up with a set of rules for myself: Do not be tempted by reviews that are too emotional and peppered with exclamations – *what an amazing book!* – and instead trust objective reviews that provide a good synopsis and a selection of quotes from the book. That said, I still get tempted when someone goes, 'Wow, this book is awesome!'

A good book review helps to elevate the reading experience. You might gain a new perspective, and if you haven't read the book yet, it can serve as a reading guide. My favourite reviews are the ones that make me think, *I've never thought of looking at it this way.* And I'll be extra motivated to read the book to see if it is truly as good as the reviewer says.

I especially enjoy Shin Hyeong-cheol's book reviews, which are detailed yet easy to read. His book, *Communal Feelings*, reads to me like an excellent collection of book reviews, but he calls it creative non-fiction. Shin writes the following about 'Cathedral', from Raymond Carver's short-story collection of the same name:

... [P]rejudice doesn't always have to be negative. It can refer to a certain way we think or act because we haven't experienced something for ourselves ... How then do we break out of our prejudice? Many novels ask this question. But rarely does any work of fiction describe the process in this level of detail.[1]

That last sentence! How could anyone not be curious? It's time to run to the nearest bookshop, grab a copy and zoom right into the last story. It's as if I'm also there in the room, feeling the tension in the air between the narrator, his wife, and her blind friend, Robert. At first, the two men look like they will never become friends, but when the wife goes to bed first, an almost unimaginable scene unfolds. And true to Shin's review, we get to watch the two men break down their differences.

43

Write Book Reviews

Six years ago, I started a blog. I set it to private mode and wrote whatever I wanted – little happenings in my life stitched together, quotes from books I'd read, some thoughts while reading … Sometimes it's just a short paragraph or two, but because I love seeing the number of posts grow, I made it a point to write every day after work.

I kept up with the habit for a year and one day. I found myself wondering: *Have I become a good writer? What would others think if they read my posts?* At that time, I was reading *The Ultimate Bibliophile – Homo Bookus*[1] by book critic Lee Kwonwoo. I happened to see that he was teaching a writing class, so I signed up immediately. For the first time in a while, my heart thrummed with excitement.

I enjoyed the two-month course so much that I ended up taking more courses for a total of six months. In class, we read a book every fortnight. In the first week, we'd take turns to share how the book made us feel, and in week two, we workshopped our writing pieces. Because we had limited time, we could only discuss four or five pieces each time, and mine was always picked. Most people were shy about sharing their work, whereas I loved getting comments. Maybe that was why Lee would pick mine every time.

We were free to write about anything we wanted. It could be a small moment in our daily life, our thoughts or feelings, as long as the flow was logical and we drew some links back to the book. You don't have to write a detailed analysis or critique of the book, Lee told us. That's the job of a book critic. Instead, write about how the book made you feel.

In other words, a reader's response. In his book *Learning to Write Begins with Reading a Book: A Writing Course*, Lee defines a reader's response as such:

> The focus isn't on the book, but on the reader, and your experience reading it. It's not stressful or challenging to write.[2]

Writing is about giving shape to our thoughts and feelings, and through the process, better understanding ourselves. Writing a reader's response is a way of reflecting on our personal experiences through a book, and as we write down our thoughts, they gain form, logic, and persuasion. Now, I don't only read to understand; I read to write. And that's how I found another motivation to keep reading.

What should I write? How do I craft my sentences? When I keep these thoughts in mind, suddenly I'm noticing many meaningful quotes and turns of phrase, which I eagerly mark out with a pencil. Imagine someone reading Han Kang's *The Vegetarian* because it won the Man Booker International Prize (now the International Booker Prize) and someone else reading the book intending to write about why Yeong-hye wants to become a plant. It's likely that the latter person is a more careful reader, because they'll not want to miss out any detail.

Writing is not easy. When I first started, I thought that it was the hardest thing on earth. How is it so difficult to craft a sentence, and then figure out how to make everything flow? But don't put pressure on yourself. The first thing to do is to get used to the action of 'writing'. If we're expressing ourselves honestly, a few sentences can also be a complete piece of work. Keep going.

When you've become used to writing, try using a prompt and set a small goal for yourself. For example, to write a one-pager on the book's strengths, or to write about how this book makes you feel, but as a fun twist, to make it as objective as possible. It's challenging, for sure. But one day, you may even think that writing is more fun than reading. But don't worry that you'd ever stop reading! Writing and reading go hand in hand.

44

The Characters' Charms

When I read, I care very much about the characters. I may not remember everyone, but once I've committed their names to my memory, they will always remain in my mind – *The Outsider*'s Meursault, Bartleby in 'Bartleby, the Scrivener', Zorba of *Zorba the Greek* and Gregor Samsa in *The Metamorphosis*. When someone I knew labelled Meursault as a 'crazy psychopath', I shrugged – to each their own! – but in my heart I thought I wouldn't want to see that person ever again. Meursault doesn't bother defending himself and I find that absolutely charming.

It's also the way Murakami describes his characters that made me have a soft spot for him. In his travel essay *Distant Drums*, Murakami describes his time on the island Spetses, and it's clear that he has a keen eye for observing people. *As expected of a novelist*, I thought. He wrote about the 'Zorba Greeks' on the island, who were watching the women sunbathing. It's these small moments that get my heart.

One of my friends was reading Hermann Hesse's *Narcissus and Goldmund* around the same time I was, and just for fun, we called each other Narcissus and Goldmund because the characters were very close to our real-life personalities.

In Hope Jahren's *Lab Girl*, Jahren and her partner nickname someone after a fictional character. Most readers won't take a second look at the following sentence, but I underlined it: 'We decided that he lived in the attic of the building and started calling him "Boo Radley"'.[1] (Boo Radley is the recluse character in Harper Lee's *To Kill A Mockingbird*.)

Have you ever felt that the people in books are more real? I do. I know precious little about the life of a friend I met yesterday, yet I can feel so deeply for a fictional character that my heart aches. A good writer fleshes out their characters, their speech, action and personalities, making it easy to feel a connection to them. They come alive in my mind.

When I read Cho Hae-jin's *I Met Loh Kiwan*, I 'met' Loh in the pages. Loh Kiwan, twenty years old, 159 cm, 47 kg. A stateless illegal immigrant. A refugee, a wandering soul from a country whose citizens were stripped of fundamental rights. Loh tries to seek asylum in Brussels, but he isn't exactly welcomed with open arms. Through the narrator's description, I picture the vast sadness and despair Loh is facing:

Turning into a deserted alleyway, he finally allowed himself to slump against a stone wall and sob uncontrollably. I stood at the end of the alleyway ... helplessly; at the same time I was straining my entire being to burn the image into my mind.[2]

Most of us wear a mask to hide our true feelings, but in novels, no one hides themselves. Their raw honesty, in turn, makes me aware of what I'm hiding behind a facade. For the next few days, I kept Loh in my thoughts, and my heart went out to all the Loh Kiwans in the world.

45

Organise Your Bookcase

Reading Fumio Sasaki's *Goodbye, Things* and Azuma Kanako's *The Ultimate Minimal Life*[1] made me conscious of all the impulse buys that were taking up too much space in my cramped room. It was time to declutter. The keyboard that I no longer used, dresses I hadn't worn for years, a desk lamp from ten years earlier, souvenirs from various holidays – everything went into the bin.

I spent the next two days organising my bookcase. First, I packed all the self-help books on success and positive mindset into boxes. Then I took out the novels and essay collections that I was unlikely to read again and in no time, I had filled several boxes.

Now came the difficult part. What about the books that I couldn't decide whether to keep or put away? I decided to empty the entire bookcase and stack everything in a neutral spot – on the floor. One by one, I decided their fate. It was straightforward: if I didn't remember anything about the book, had no desire to read it now and was unlikely to read it in the future, it went into a box. If I hesitated, I'd ask myself once more, *Will I read this again?* If the answer was a no, it went into the box, albeit with some reluctance.

It didn't matter if the book was a global bestseller or not. I decided to prioritise myself: I wanted to keep books that I would read, not what others were interested in. Not books that were all the rage, but books that were important to me. I wanted my bookcase to be a reflection of my past, present and future. I'd trim my collection to 500 books – not too many, not too few. And I'd only keep the books I needed.

When I first learnt that the famed Japanese bibliophile Takashi Tachibana had a 'Cat Building' that housed more than 200,000 books, I was in awe. I can't afford a building, but I would love a spacious reading room lined with bookcases. Wouldn't it be awesome if I could find any book I wanted in my own home?

But after reading several books written by bibliophiles, I realised that maybe that isn't the life for me. I love buying books, but bibliophiles take book-buying to the extreme.

In *The Pain of a Bibliophile* (what a title!), it's said that around half – or maybe more – of bibliophiles buy books every day, and because of that, they barely have space to walk in their own house. It takes about 10,000 books to open a secondhand bookshop, and Japanese author Takeshi Okazaki keeps about 20,000 or 30,000 books at home. One of the bibliophiles interviewed in the book estimated owning about 30,000 books, but when the actual count turned out to be 130,000, they chuckled shamefacedly.

Despite owning a whole lot more books, the author claims that 500 is the ideal number of books to have at home. A true-blue bibliophile should have a sizeable collection, yet have the flexibility to adjust it according to one's changing preferences. The author quotes a literary scholar saying, *More isn't better.* I imagined a room filled with several hundred of my favourite books displayed neatly, with their spines visible. From then on, I stopped having the ridiculous idea to fill every inch of my house with books.

In those two days, I pushed out more than ten boxes of books, but within a few months, my shelves are packed again. Even though I resolved to buy only the books I need, the problem is that when I'm shopping online, every book looks like something I need. That's why I keep the number '500' in mind, treating it as a symbol of significance. I should keep only what I need. After all, I will spend my entire life curating an ever-evolving collection of books I love. Buy less, read more.

46

Read Books Like an 'Axe'

When I was reading *A Mother's Reckoning: Living in the Aftermath of the Columbine Tragedy* by Sue Klebold, I found myself wanting to give up several times. I started crying three paragraphs into the book, and I lost count of how many times in the early chapters that I continued to tear up. In 1999, the Columbine High School massacre sent shockwaves across America. Two students shot twelve fellow students dead, and injured more than twenty, including a victim who passed away in 2025 as a result of her injuries from the shooting. Sue Klebold was the mother of one of the perpetrators, Dylan Klebold.

In the aftermath of the shooting, the two students were condemned as monstrous abominations, and their parents accused of being abusers that turned them into killers. But Sue Klebold insists that her son didn't have violent tendencies. In fact, he was affectionate and considerate. Sue and her husband, Tom, had nicknamed their son 'Sunshine Boy', and unlike what the world thought, they were ordinary, loving parents. Sixteen years after the massacre, she tells us a hard truth through her book: the tragedy could have happened to anyone.

'This book is the epitome of darkness.' 'Reading it makes me uncomfortable.' 'As a parent, it's horrifying to read this.' 'I want to run away from the book.' Most of the reviews said similar things.

Why then, do we have to read about the tragedy? Why do we have to know that the two teenagers weren't monsters, and they weren't deprived of familial love? Why do we have to remember that anyone can be a perpetrator, and that it could've happened to any parent? My answer is this – because it's the hard truth.

It's not going to be a light or easy read. But we shouldn't run away. Many truths in the world are hard-hitting. If you need something easy and comforting, there are self-help books. But there are times we need to learn to live with discomfort.

'Don't run away,' I remind myself. I tend to stay in my comfort zone, and reading is my way of pushing myself beyond that. Stereotypes or biases aren't easy to break; I want to grow into a more mature person.

'A book must be the axe for the frozen sea inside,' Franz Kafka wrote to his friend Oscar Pollak in January 1904.

'Axe' is a scary word, but Kafka believes that reading should make us uncomfortable. Earlier in his letter to Pollak, he writes:

> I think we ought to read only the kind of books that wound and stab us ... we need books that affect us like a disaster, that grieve us deeply, like the death of someone we love more than ourselves ...[1]

Otherwise, we can neither see truth nor reality.

47

Read Books That You're
Interested In

Three summers ago, I decided that I would devote my days to the craft of writing, in the hope that I could become a full-time writer one day. Last summer, I sat down at my desk as usual, but in the sweltering heat I couldn't write at all. The moment I sat down in my chair, I started spacing out. My mind and body seemed to exist in separate dimensions, and I was growing more listless by the day. A sudden inspiration hit me. If I couldn't write, why not do something similar? I decided to spend my days reading about writing, and I pored over my books with renewed enthusiasm.

I stacked all the books I owned about the craft of writing on my desk and bed. Some spines still uncracked, others I'd read. There was so much I was curious about. Do these accomplished authors also experience writer's block? Have they ever looked at their own work and thought, *Oh God, what did I just write*? Are they born with a flair for writing? Would they think I was reckless for wanting to be a professional author? I devoured dozens of books, getting different answers each time. Gradually, my interest expanded to reading about the lives of those who work in the arts. After all, writers aren't the only group of people engaging in creative pursuits.

Earlier this year, I discovered the work of Japanese illustrator Mizumaru Anzai. Most people would know Anzai for having worked with Murakami, but to his colleagues, Anzai was a brilliant artist, and one could even argue that it was his illustrations that complemented Murakami's writing perfectly. The book *Mizumaru Anzai*, published three years after his passing, offered much insight into his unique way of looking at art, and in particular, the following quote from his student caught my attention:

He will work on a painting that he thinks will be 'good' until the point where he thinks it's 'good' and only stop when he truly believes it's 'good'. That's Mizumaru Anzai for you. He doesn't say, 'I'm going to paint something that surprises or shocks' or 'I want to make everyone smile'. He only paints what he believes is 'good' … He wants to create art that he'll be confident to show the world, and that, to him, is the most persuasive piece of art.[1]

What's important isn't what others think, but to believe in ourselves, our feelings, our abilities. I aspire to be like this. Now that I think back, I had been consumed by the fear that people would figure out that I couldn't write. Instead of running away, I should take a leaf from Anzai's book.

Mizumaru Anzai was my favourite read in 2017. The stories of writers and artists felt close to my heart, and I finished one book after another.

Dear reader, what are you interested in these days? Quitting your job? Moving to another country? AI? Or are your thoughts still lingering on the person who left you? Your partner whom you can't seem to understand? Are you feeling unconfident about yourself? As though there's too much on your mind? Or are your thoughts dwelling on someone or something you've been reading about – the king in a historical drama? Jane Austen? Yuval Noah Harari? Feminism?

Or maybe you haven't been sleeping well. Someone you hate is taking up too much of your headspace. Have you been crying first thing in the morning? Or perhaps you've been feeling disillusioned about your job. You want to live your life and go elsewhere – open a small art studio, set up a one-man publisher, find happiness in the little things in life.

Whatever it is, the book that truly understands us is somewhere in the bookshop waiting for us, waiting for you.

48

Read Beyond What You're Interested In

A few years ago, I read several books by Peter Drucker. My dad, deeply impressed by Drucker's theories on modern management, had insisted that I read him. I did so reluctantly, but despite my initial misgivings, it wasn't boring at all. I might not have understood all the jargon, but I enjoyed the logical flow of Drucker's prose so much that I ended up buying his autobiography – *Adventures of a Bystander*.

I was impressed. Drucker didn't have the stereotypical rigidity of a so-called expert. He was very accepting of the world and others. Despite being known as the 'father' of modern management, he didn't insist on looking at things through a single lens, not even in his field of expertise.

Drucker was an avid learner. Every few years or so, he'd pick up something new, and his areas of interest were so varied that one can't help but wonder how a busy management consultant like himself could find the time to do so many things. Statistics, medieval history, Japanese art, economics. As he expanded his interests, he was also learning to observe the world from a fresh perspective. He wasn't just a scholar of business management – he was a guru.

Reading Drucker taught me that there are times we have to step away from the issue in order to address it, and that it's important to keep learning. Rebecca Solnit captures it perfectly:

> … [S]ometimes the way back into the heart of the question begins by going outward and beyond.[1]

Jump over the boundaries that you've set for yourself and step into the wider world. And when you're doing that, leave aside your problems and take the time to see new things, form new and deep connections.

Wouldn't it be nice if we could travel anytime we wanted to? But for most of us, that's hard, so we read. Reading lets us leave ourselves behind and explore the bigger world out there. There isn't a need to feel like we have to accomplish much out there. With just a slight change in mood, we'll be able to live today as a different person from yesterday.

Some say those who read are idealistic. Perhaps they are on their exploration of the world. Why must we always be 'realistic'? Sometimes it takes a little escape from reality to make our lives a tiny bit better.

49

Read to Overcome Despair

A friend who'd taught students ranging from grade 1 to 12 once told me, 'It's not easy to motivate the kids to study. Even the top students in high school are saying things like, *I'm going to move to Germany in the future. How about the rest of you? The Netherlands, or somewhere else?* See? In the end, it doesn't matter if you're good at studies or not. Everyone finds it hard to be happy in Korea.'

It's not just the teenagers. Another friend, who was twenty-seven, told me what happened at his class reunion: 'Guess what? Everyone was saying that we should just move to a different country together. It's impossible to survive here. You'd think those lucky ones who got full-time permanent positions are doing fine, but in fact, everyone's miserable.' That reminded me of Chang Kang-myong's novel *Because I Hate Korea*. Gye-na, the main female character, wants to move to Australia.

Life also doesn't get better with age. My friend's older friends, my elder sister and her husband's friends all have plans to move to a different country or have already done so. I have a friend who hates the rat race, and the only reason she works hard to earn money is to move abroad. 'Once I have enough money, no matter how old I am then, I'm going to move to a place where I can live with more dignity,' she told me. And some time back, another friend suddenly moved to Vietnam. He didn't even have any confirmed plans before moving; he was that desperate.

In the novel, Gye-na says that it's impossible to be happy when one lives in fear of the future. I absolutely get it. There was a period of time I kept talking about moving to Sweden. I know it's not so simple, but whenever life was crumbling, I'd search for universities in Sweden. I shortlisted the city and the university I was interested in and went to read up more about it. Even if it was just a dream, I needed something to ease the dreariness of reality.

Life is like a pendulum swinging between utter despair and a reluctant acceptance of fate. We live under the bleakness that society imposes on us. If we don't make an effort to find joy in our daily lives, there's only depression waiting for us. We live in an odd space where being positive about the future is seen as naïve, whereas expecting the worst is wise. A life where the day starts with exhaustion. Since when have we become used to such misery?

I find myself crying more often. I cry because I am sad, and because I am emotional. Strangely, I've become an even more emotional person than before. Darkness seems to blanket life like an algae bloom, and I rub my eyes hard for a glimmer of hope. I turn towards books, as if that's the most natural thing to do. I collect sentences that speak of hope. I engrave the scenes in my eyes. Over and over again, I keep comforting myself that darkness hasn't swallowed the entire world.

Kim Keum Hee asks the following question in the author's note for *Too Bright Outside for Love*:

> When things get rough, is it a sign of weakness if we only try our best to get through the day? But is it right in the first place that the day feels so heavy?[1]

I agree with Kim. I would choose 'weakness' to get over a rough patch. But I'm not going to blame myself for a hard day. I will do best to live the day well and I will keep dreaming. Even if it feels impossible, I'll do my best to hold on to a glimmer of hope. Even if it looks silly, I will allow myself to feel, to cry, as I look forward to a future where hope, not despair, is in abundance.

Whenever I need a little hope, I think of the following lines from Italo Calvino's *Invisible Cities*:

The inferno of the living is not something that will be ... seek and learn to recognise who and what, in the midst of inferno, are not inferno, then make them endure, give them space.[2]

50

Read Difficult Books

I like my reading list to get progressively more challenging. Sometimes, I'll plunge straight into a particularly difficult book, but most of the time I prefer to just let my mind be stretched a little.

But singer-songwriter Ehosuk, who is also my friend, made me rethink my strategy. His album, aptly titled *Philosophy of Secondees*, caught my attention because of its philosophical and mature lyrics. Once, he told me he enjoys reading philosophy books and his favourite author is Jean-Paul Sartre. Naturally, I thought he had grew up a voracious reader. But I later learnt that he had only started reading in the past couple of years. When I asked how he could read such difficult books in such a short time, he gave an interesting answer:

When I was penning my lyrics, I thought to myself, *I should read some books*. Because I don't have the habit of reading, any book is difficult for me. I didn't think much and jumped straight into *Thus Spoke Zarathustra* by Friedrich Nietzsche. Oh God, I didn't understand a single thing! I seriously thought it's the kind of book an average person reads, so I was very upset that I had no idea what was going on. But I pushed myself to keep reading and after that, I read a book analysing Sartre's works. I got so into existentialism that I bought one of Sartre's books. I had no idea what I was reading at first, but slowly I got the gist of it.

I was in awe. *So it's possible to read like this.* I was inching my way out of my comfort zone while Ehosuk simply jumped in at the deep end. I imagined him mulling over each sentence. Perhaps he would only read a few pages a day and revisit an earlier part again because he had no idea what was going on. It must have been a struggle and a chore, but his persistence paid off.

That's a great way to handle difficult books. Instead of being ambitious and insisting on understanding 100 per cent, take the pressure off yourself. Keep going, even if you're just doing a few pages a day. Step beyond 'I want to read a book by this author' to 'I'm reading their book now'. So what if you can't understand everything? You're reading, and that's what matters.

If we keep going, will we be able to understand the text one day? Japanese philosopher Tatsuru Uchida would

probably say yes. In an article in the Korean literary magazine *Mindle*, Uchida talks about 'reading physically':

> I am translating Emmanuel Levinas, but when I first
> read his book, it was so difficult I barely understood
> anything ... For two weeks, I read without compre-
> hending, but strangely enough, I was starting to be in
> sync with the flow of the sentences. 'There's a question
> mark coming.' 'I bet he's ending on this turn of phrase.'
> I was moving in tandem with his breathing and, at the
> same time, starting to understand his thoughts and
> what he wants to express.[1]

No matter how difficult a book is, if we keep reading
it over and over, our body will be the first to react to it,
and at some point, it clicks. I imagine the physical text
encircling our bodies before seeping into our brains.
Uchida doesn't offer an explanation for why our bodies
react faster than our minds, but it doesn't matter. What's
important is that it is indeed happening. When reading
difficult books, have trust in the process and keep going.
You'll come to realise no book is too difficult.

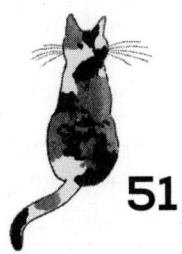

51

Read Books That Preserve Your Sense of Self

The film *Detachment*, hailed as an exposé of the American education system, is also very much about the anxiety and loneliness every individual faces, in the sense of *I'm falling apart myself; how do I save you?* Henry, played by Adrien Brody, is a teacher, but he is in dire need of help, more so than his students. No one in the movie is happy and whole, but we still get some uplifting moments when the characters extend a helping hand or a word of comfort to one another.

These are teenagers in the spring of their life, yet they've already lost their passion. Henry suggests that they learn to read aloud, and with emotion. He tells them – and us – to fight against things that are blunting our emotions and manipulating the way we think, like the ads we see every day that brainwash us into subscribing to a certain image of happiness, that we have to look gorgeous, be thin, be famous, keep up with the trends. Henry says we must shield ourselves from these external influences. Happiness is in our minds, our senses, and our own beliefs. And reading will help.

When I hear the emotion and the urgency in Henry's voice, I can't help but think of Austrian philosopher Ivan Illich's *The Right to Useful Unemployment*. I can absolutely imagine Adrien Brody doing the narration. In fact, I am convinced that he would be the best person to bring out the essence of the book – Illich's anger and sorrow as he laments the intrusion of media and consumerism in our lives.

> The now soporific, now raucous intrusion of the media reaches deeply into the commune, the village, the corporation, the school. The sounds made by the editors and announcers of programmed texts daily pervert the words of a spoken language into building blocks for packaged messages. Today, one must either be isolated and cut off, or a carefully guarded, affluent drop-out, to allow one's children to play in an environment where they listen to people rather than to stars, speakers, or instructors.[1]

According to Illich, society fosters a consumerist mind-set and diminishes the self in the process. The beauty of individualism is lost, like a field of spring flowers wilted to a dull grey. It becomes harder to find satisfaction and happiness in life.

That's why we should read books that preserve our sense of self. Not just to buy books, but to read them and understand the world. Instead of blindly following what the media tells us, we should find our own happiness. When we're feeling lonely, we shouldn't head to a shop but visit a friend. When we crave stability, instead of dreaming of a perfect home, we should find perfection in a simple life within our means.

Be aware of our own anxieties, know how to prioritise ourselves, understand and manage our inner desires, and books will help us find our way forward.

The media is full of sensationalised stories and temptations. To fight against its influence, we need to build a 'story vending machine' for ourselves. Each time we need something to lift our spirits, we can pick a story and let it play in our hearts.

When I feel a pang of deprivation looking at an ostentatiously rich house, I'll dispense the story of *Living the Good Life* by the couple Helen and Scott Nearing – a book about finding happiness in a simple life. When I'm sick of the way society dictates how we view success, I remind myself of Somerset Maugham's *The Moon and Sixpence*, about a man who bravely pursues his dream even though his method is questionable. Leo Tolstoy's *Anna Karenina* teaches us the importance of prioritising our own feelings. That's my go-to story when I struggle with despising what the ads say yet yearning to fit into the mould. And that's why I read: to collect stories that'll help me be myself.

52

What Have You Been Reading?

One time, I texted my close friends and family to ask what they'd been reading recently and their thoughts about that book. It was a completely random question, but thankfully, no one was annoyed. Some asked for a few days to mull over it, but everyone responded with sincerity.

B wrote me a long reply, yet at the same time apologising for not being of much help. She told me she had recently read Alain de Botton's *The Course of Love*. 'I've been struggling with balancing my identity as a mother of two and wanting to be wholly myself again. Sometimes it feels like I'm fading away while motherhood takes over my entire identity. But I feel so guilty for having these thoughts. I keep asking myself: *Am I being an irresponsible mother?* You can't imagine my relief when I read the book. It's as if it knew exactly what I was going through. I felt understood. I'm not the only one who thinks this way. My feelings are valid.'

Friend C, who is a mum of three and organises a monthly book club, said she had read *Kim Jiyoung, Born in 1982* by Cho Nam-ju. 'It helps me take a step back to objectively look at what I had thought were my "responsibilities". All the things I was supposed to do just because I'm a woman. How is it that I readily accept everything as my obligation? Now, I'm no longer sure. What does it mean to be a woman?'

D, who is constantly worrying about something, shared her thoughts on *The Lady with the Dog* by Anton Chekhov. 'It's a gripping collection; we see the dark side of humanity, the raw anxiety. The characters make me realise that perhaps I don't have to put up a perfect facade in life. Life doesn't have to be a bed of roses. It's a good reminder that each of us is a unique individual. And these days, I've been thinking about how to live my life.'

E, who is busy preparing for the ancestor rites ceremony, sent her husband's answer instead. I've met her husband, an affable man with a deep voice who likes to crack jokes. He said he recently read Kim Ho-dong's historical atlas series – the volume on Central Eurasia.[1] 'Seeing how people in the past used to travel great distances makes me think that perhaps life isn't just about staying put in one spot for the rest of our lives.'

F, who is a documentary director, recently read *Voices from Chernobyl* by Svetlana Alexievich. 'It narrates a truly horrifying incident. There was so much I hadn't known.

I respect the author; she risked her life to bring these stories to the world. And it gets me thinking about how to tell someone's stories and to capture their voices.'

G, who is a generous soul and always has something for us when we meet, said she just read Kim Seonju's *Etiquettes in Parting*.[2] 'I love the self-reflections in this one. Instead of blaming materialism, we need to look into ourselves instead.'

H, who quit her job to spend some time on Jeju Island, enjoyed Jean-Jacques Sempé's *Sincères amitiés*.[3] 'Friendship is more challenging than love. It's all in the details, yet many things aren't spelled out. Friendship demands care, but also distance. The book makes me realise that I'm not the only one who finds it hard. But despite the doubt and uncertainty, all of us still crave genuine friendship.'

J, who's always fun to chat with, read Paul Kalanithi's *When Breath Becomes Air*. 'We live as though life will go on for ever, but death is always hovering. Kalanithi gave it his all in life, and when he was diagnosed with final-stage cancer at a young age, he faced death bravely. He knew what he wanted and what was important to him, so he lived with passion until his last breath. It makes me wonder how I should live my life, so that when the moment of death comes, I can say that I've lived a good life.'

K, who always faces life's challenges head-on and writes poetry, told me that the following book was a huge inspiration. 'In *Study of Science*,[4] Kim Sangwook points out that we think of Shakespeare or Socrates as general knowledge, and asks why we don't view scientific discoveries in the same way. For someone who is more of an "arts person", this book teaches useful nuggets of basic science.'

L, who is about to return to work after a year of maternity leave, said she learnt a lot from Venerable Pomnyun Sunim's *Lessons for Mothers*.[5]

M, who is juggling motherhood and her career, and doesn't want to quit the job she loves even though we think she has lost quite a bit of weight recently, said a book that had helped her a lot was Gong Ji-young's *I Was Alone Like a Raindrop*.[6] 'When I went on a business trip to San Diego, I was having a hard time mentally. The stories in the book made me feel less lonely.'

I asked my family the same question. My sister told me about a book that her bibliophile friend lent her – Mari Yonehara's *The Deep Red Truth of Anya the Liar*, which goes by the title of *Prague's Girls' Generation*[7] in the Korean edition. 'The book tells the stories of people who lived in the communist system. The author, who was Japanese, was searching for classmates she'd studied with in Prague forty years before. All three friends had parents who were communists. Anya, her friend from Romania, claims to believe in communism, where everyone lives equally, but she herself is living a bourgeois life. It's so frustrating that she doesn't realise how different her words and actions are. She only sees what she wants to see, and it's hard to root for someone like that.' My brother-in-law also sent his response through my sister. While he didn't read it recently, he really liked Nanami Shiono's *Stories of the Romans*.[8] 'The battle scenes are good.'

My mum recently read Lee Kwang-sik's *Stories of the Universe for Insomniac Nights*.[9] She'd been raving about the book, but when I asked her what it was that made the deepest impression, her answer was surprisingly short. 'Besides hydrogen, the elements that make up our bodies were created when a star exploded. Same for stones, leaves and birds. Isn't that cool?' My dad visited the Shin Dong-yeop House and Museum in Buyeo County not long ago. After coming home, he reread *The Complete Works of Shin Dong-yeop*.[10] 'In his poem "Go Away, Shell", he speaks of his intense desire for the pretence and falsehood that pervade society to disappear, leaving behind purity in knowledge-seeking. I'm already in my mid-sixties and it makes me wonder if I've managed to live a life free from facades and empty formalities.'

The last person who replied to me was N. She said when she got my question, she spent a few days thinking about Primo Levi, a Jewish Italian chemist and Holocaust survivor, and asking herself, 'Why did Levi leave such a deep impression on me?' N said that for a period of time, she used Levi's prisoner number, 174517, as her password, and each time she typed it out, she'd think of Levi. 'From him, I learnt that to carelessly judge a person and their situation is violence. I think it's rare to meet someone like Levi, who makes the effort to really understand the complexities of humanity. That's why I love his writing. I bashfully recommend it to everyone around me, as if I'm confessing my love. When I got your question, I was thinking about *The Drowned and the Saved* in particular, because it was Levi's last work before his death. But if you ask me again today, I'll want to tell you about *The Periodic Table*. You get it, don't you? It's impossible to pick one.'

To me, N was like Levi. I've never seen her talk carelessly about anyone, and even if she's trying to change the mood, she never cracks jokes at the expense of others. There are some books we meet in life that feel like falling in love; we think of them all the time, just like N with Levi. And when such books touch something deep inside our hearts, it feels like we're reading them afresh each day.

The question 'What have you been reading?' seems to have the power to open a latch in our hearts. The moment we welcome books into ourselves, we're bravely opening the door to our hearts. We confess our loneliness, our weaknesses, uncertainties and worries as we open up about the values and worldviews that each of us holds close to our hearts. The doorway to self-reflection that's hidden inside us opens, and we grow to become a person who understands introspection. When everyone else is asking 'What movie did you watch recently?' and 'What drama are you watching now?', I want to ask, 'What book have you been reading?' I hope to make a space, however small, for books in our conversations. I want to open the latch in my heart when I'm with you.

53

If Books Disappeared from the World

Ray Bradbury's *Fahrenheit 451* paints a dystopian world where books no longer exist. The last few bibliophiles desperately hide books in their basements or inside ventilation ducts, but their houses are burned down, and they are branded as criminals. The story follows Guy Montag, a 'fireman' whose job is to destroy books, and how he re-evaluates his entire life after meeting Clarisse McClellan, a teenager who loves books.

Reading the book, I can't help but imagine – *What if books disappeared from the world?* Authors would disappear alongside the books. Does that mean future generations would not know Park Wan-suh, Yi Cheong-jun, Virginia Woolf, Ernest Hemingway and George Orwell? It would mean losing these people who've dedicated their lives to their area of study and have put in such painful effort to write, and also losing the stories that they've written, stories of the deepest and rawest humanity that one might find hard to tell aloud.

If books were to disappear, no one would know what *The Veritable Records of the Joseon Dynasty* was. There wouldn't be textbooks. Records of humanity before the advent of photography and videography would vanish. Few stories are passed down by word of mouth, so only the rare few would still remember that Socrates was determined and resolute, even at the moment of death. If books were to disappear, people would also stop thinking about passing down discoveries and ideas to the next generation. Each of us would be stuck in our narrow experience of life, and it would be difficult to imagine what's out there in the world.

The good quotes, famous lines and creative thoughts abundant on the internet would also vanish. Because most of them come from books. The posts on my favourite Facebook page, 'Fuelling Passion', are usually synopses of books, so it means that page would be gone too. While there are still other ways to learn and share experiences, like TV talk shows, they lack depth in interpretation, analysis and insight.

Argentine writer Jorge Luis Borges is widely quoted as having said that while some cannot imagine a world without birds, or a world without water, he is unable to imagine a world without books.

In a text titled 'A Letter to Borges', Susan Sontag responds to his sentiment by saying:

Some people think of reading only as a kind of escape: an escape from the 'real' everyday world to an imaginary world, the world of books. Books are much more. They are a way of being fully human.[1]

American author Andrew Piper, who I believe must have read Borges, says: 'I can imagine a world without books. I cannot imagine one without reading.'[2]

I sat up straighter when I read this line. Indeed, if books disappeared, readers would exist no more. That means a part of me would disappear. I, who spend hours leafing through pages, annotating with a pencil, so completely absorbed that it's past midnight when I finally get up to turn off the lights. I, who am always curious to know what a person is reading, especially if I'm meeting them for the first time, and while I may be too shy to ask, the thought will continue to linger in my mind even after I come home. Because I feel closer to people who've read the same book as me than to people I've known for years, I often recommend books to my friends. Books bring colour to my simple life and if I have a book in my hands, it feels like I'm always connected with the world. Whether I'm bored, lonely, upset or depressed, books soothe me and everything feels all right again. What would I do without books?

I can't imagine a world without books. Until my last breath, I want to live my life reading, always.

NOTES

1. READ BESTSELLERS

1   Ichiro Kishimi and Fumitake Koga, *The Courage to Be Disliked* (Allen & Unwin, 2018).

2. READ BEYOND BESTSELLERS

1   Nicolas Bouvier, translated by Robyn Marsack, *The Way of the World* (Eland & Sickle Moon Books, 2007).

3. READ ON THE TRAIN

1   류시화, 지구별 여행자 (김영사, 2002).

4. READ SMALL BOOKS

1   이기준, 저, 죄송한데요 (민음사, 2016).

6. UNDERLINING AND ANNOTATIONS

1   Translated from the Korean edition: 파트리크쥐스킨트, (역) 김인순, 깊이의 강요(깊이에의 강요, 2002).

7. ALWAYS HAVE A BOOK WITH YOU

1   Translated from the Korean edition: 나카지마 요시미치, (역) 심성녕, 비사교적 사교성 (바다출판시, 2016).

8. CHOOSE BOOKS, NOT THE INTERNET

1 Nicholas Carr, *The Shallows: What the Internet is Doing to Our Brains* (Atlantic Books, 2010). Quoting from: William James, *The Principles of Psychology*, vol. 1 (New York: Holt, 1890), pp. 104–6. Translation of Dumont's essay is from James E. Black and William T. Greenough, 'Induction of Pattern in Neural Structure by Experience: Implications for Cognitive Development', in *Advances in Developmental Psychology*, vol. 4, ed. Michael E. Lamb, Ann L. Brown, and Barbara Rogoff (Erlbaum, 1986).

9. USE A TIMER APP

1 Translated from the Korean edition:알렉스 륄레, (역) 김태정, 달콤한 로그아웃 (나무위의책, 2013)

10. READ CLASSICS

1 Italo Calvino, translated by Martin McLaughlin, *Why Read the Classics?* (Penguin Books, 2009.).

11. READ NOVELS

1 Herman Melville, *Great Short Works of Herman Melville* (HarperCollins, 2009).

12. READ POETRY

1 황인찬, 이이체, 이우성, 유계영, 안희연 저 외 7명, 나는 매번 시 쓰기가 재미있다 (서랍의날씨, 2016).
2 은유, 싸울 때마다 투명해진다 (서해문집, 2016).
3 김승희, 희망이 외롭다 (문학동네, 2012).

14. BED, NIGHT AND LIGHTS

1 정혜윤, 침대와 책 (웅진지식하우스, 2007).

15. FAVOURITE AUTHOR

1 Paul Auster, *The Brooklyn Follies* (Faber & Faber, 2005).

16. BOOKS AND DRINKS

1 정인성, 소설 마시는 시간 (나무, 나무, 2016).

17. YOU DON'T ALWAYS HAVE TO FINISH IT

1 Henry David Thoreau, *Walden, or Life in the Woods* (Vintage Classics, 2007).

18. ARE BOOKS USEFUL?

1 Michel de Montaigne, translated by Charles Cotton and edited by W. Carew Hazlitt, *Essays* (London Reeves and Turner, 1877).

19. VISITING THE LIBRARY

1 Jean-Paul Sartre, translated by Robert Baldick, *Nausea* (Penguin Classics, 2000).
2 Alberto Manguel, *The Library at Night* (Vintage, 2011).

20. THE JOY OF COLLECTING QUOTES

1 Seneca, translated by C. D. N. Costa, *On the Shortness of Life* (Penguin, 2004).
2 Translated from the Korean edition: 괴테, 파우스트 (민음사, 1999).
3 Translated by the Korean edition: 조영래, 전태일 평전, (아름다 운선태일, 2009).
4 Albert Einstein, *Ideas and Opinions* (Broadway Books, 2010).
5 Mark Rowlands, *The Philosopher and the Wolf* (Granta Books, 2009).

6 신영복, 감옥으로부터의 사색 (돌베개, 1998).

7 Annie Dillard, *The Writing Life* (HarperCollins, 1989).

8 Confucius, translated by D. C. Lau, *The Analects* (Penguin, 1979).

21. BOOK CLUBS

1 Hannah Arendt, *Eichmann in Jerusalem: A Report on the Banality of Evil* (The Viking Press, 1964).

22. READ TO SEEK ANSWERS

1 Aristotle, *Nicomachean Ethics* (Batoche Books, 1999).

2 Daniel Gilbert, *Stumbling on Happiness* (Vintage, 2006).

23. E-BOOKS

1 David Sax, *The Revenge of Analog* (PublicAffairs, 2016).

24. POCKETS OF FREE TIME

1 Patrick Süskind, translated by Michael Hofmann, *The Story of Mr Sommer* (Bloomsbury, 1992).

25. READ SLOWLY

1 Frédéric Gros, translated by John Howe, *A Philosophy of Walking* (Verso, 2014).

26. LIFE-CHANGING READS

1 최윤필, 가만한 당신 (마음산책, 2016)

2 이화경, 사랑하고 쓰고 파괴하다 (행성B, 2017).

27. INDIE BOOKSHOPS

1   김영건, 당신에게 말을 건다 (알마, 2017).

28. THE NEXT BOOK TO READ

1   금정연, 실패를 모르는 멋진 문장들 (어크로스, 2017).

29. READ WHEN YOU'RE HAPPY, WHEN YOU'RE ANXIOUS, AND IN THE MOMENTS IN BETWEEN

1   Erich Fromm, *To Have or To Be?* (Open Road Media, 2013).

30. MOVIES AND NOVELS

1   종의 기원 (은행나무, 2016).
2   정유정, 7년의 밤 (은행나무, 2011).
3   Austin Wright, *Tony and Susan* (Atlantic Books, 2010).

31. LET'S DISCUSS BOOKS

1   이덕무, 책에 미친 바보 (태학사, 2022).

34. READ BOOKS THAT RESONATE

1   Grégoire Delacourt, translated by Anthea Bell, *The First Thing You See* (Weidenfeld & Nicolson, 2015).

35. READ BEYOND SUCCESS AND FAILURE

1   김연수, 소설가의 일 (문학동네, 2014).

36. READ DURING THE HOLIDAYS

1   Holbrook Jackson, *The Anatomy of Bibliomania* (The Soncino Press, 1932).

37. THE FLAVOURS OF WORDS

1 이기호, 웬만해선 아무렇지 않다 (마음산책, 2016)
2 김혜리, 김혜리의 영화의 일기 <씨네21, 1097호>, 2017.

38. PARENTS WHO READ

1 Anne Fadiman, *Ex Libris: Confessions of a Common Reader* (Farrar, Straus and Giroux, 2011).

39. READ WIDELY, THEN DEEPLY

1 Richard Dawkins, *The Selfish Gene* (Oxford University Press, 2016).

40. KEEP A READING LIST

1 Translated from the Korean edition: 장 그르니에, (역) 김용기, 일상적인 삶 (민음사, 2020).

41. READ TO LIVE THE LIFE YOU WANT

1 정여울, 공부할 권리 (민음사, 2016).

42. READ BOOK REVIEWS

1 신형철, 느낌의공동체 (문학동네, 2011)

43. WRITE BOOK REVIEWS

1 이권우, 책읽기의 달인, 호모 부커스 (그린비, 2008).
2 이권우, 책읽기부터 시작하는 글쓰기 수업 (한겨레출판사, 2015).

44. THE CHARACTERS' CHARMS

1 Hope Jahren, *Lab Girl* (Knopf Doubleday, 2016).
2 조해진, 로기완을 만났다, (창비, 2011).

45. ORGANISE YOUR BOOKCASE

1 Translated from the Korean edition: 아즈마 가나코, (역) 박승희, 궁극의 미니멀라이프 (즐거운상상, 2016).

46. READ BOOKS LIKE AN 'AXE'

1 Franz Kafka, translated by Richard and Clara Winston, *Letters to Friends, Family, and Editors* (Knopf, 1990).

47. READ BOOKS THAT YOU'RE INTERESTED IN

1 Translated from the Korean edition: 안자이 미즈마루, (역) 권남희, 안자이미즈마루: 마음을 다해 대충 그린 그림 (씨네 21 북스, 2015).

48. READ BEYOND WHAT YOU'RE INTERESTED IN

1 Rebecca Solnit, *The Faraway Nearby* (Penguin Books, 2013).

49. READ TO OVERCOME DESPAIR

1 김금희, 너무 한낮의 연애 (문학동네, 2016).
2 Italo Calvino, translated by William Weaver, *Invisible Cities* (Vintage, 2010).

50. READ DIFFICULT BOOKS

1 Translated from the Korean edition: 우치다 다쓰루, <민들레 111호>'학교에서 가르쳐 주지 않는 것 세 가지' (민들레, 2017).

51. READ BOOKS THAT PRESERVE YOUR SENSE OF SELF

1 Ivan Illich, *The Right to Useful Unemployment* (Marion Boyars Publishers, 1996).

52. WHAT HAVE YOU BEEN READING?

1 김호동, 아틀라스 중앙유라시아사 (사계절, 2016).
2 김선주, 이별에도 예의가 필요하다 (한겨레출판, 2010).
3 Translated from the Korean edition: 장자크 상페, (역) 양영란, 진정한 우정 (열린책들, 2017).
4 김상욱, 김상욱의 과학공부 (동아시아, 2016).
5 엄마 수업, 법륜 (휴, 2011).
6 공지영, 빗방울처럼 나는 혼자였다 (오픈하우스, 2011).
7 Translated from the Korean edition: 요네하라 마리, (역) 이현진, 프라하의 소녀시대 (마음산책, 2006).
8 Translated from the Korean edition: 시오노 나나미, (역) 김석희, 로마인 이야기 (한길사, 2007).
9 이광식, 잠 안 오는 밤에 읽는 우주 토픽 (들메나무, 2016).
10 신동엽, 신동엽 전집 (창비, 2008).

53. IF BOOKS DISAPPEARED FROM THE WORLD

1 Jonathan Cott, *Susan Sontag: The Complete Rolling Stone Interview* (Yale University Press, 2013).
2 Andrew Piper, *Book Was There: Reading in Electronic Times* (University of Chicago Press, 2012).

A NOTE ON THE AUTHOR

Hwang Bo-reum is the author of the international bestseller *Welcome to the Hyunam-dong Bookshop* and the essay collections *Every Day I Read, Trying Kickboxing for the First Time, The Perfect Distance* and *Simple Living*. She lives in Seoul.

A NOTE ON THE TRANSLATOR

Shanna Tan is a literary translator working from Korean, Chinese and Japanese into English. Her translations include the bestselling *Welcome to the Hyunam-dong Bookshop* by Hwang Bo-reum. Born and raised in Singapore, she is currently spending some time in Bangkok.

A NOTE ON THE TYPE

The text of this book is set in Minion, a digital typeface designed by Robert Slimbach in 1990 for Adobe Systems. The name comes from the traditional naming system for type sizes, in which minion is between nonpareil and brevier. It is inspired by late Renaissance-era type.